Inspiring Innovation

U.S. GOVERNMENT
OFFICIAL EDITION NOTICE

Use of ISBN Prefix

Legal Status and Use of Seals and Logos

For Sale by the Superintendent of Documents, U.S. Government Printing Office
Internet: bookstore.gpo.gov. Phone: toll free (866) 512-1800; DC area (202) 512-1800
Fax: (202) 512-2104. Mail: Stop IDCC, Washington, DC 20402-00001

ISBN 978-1-935352-46-4

NAVAL WAR COLLEGE VAN BEUREN STUDIES IN LEADERSHIP AND ETHICS NO. 1

The John A. van Beuren Studies in Leadership and Ethics series of publications was established to advance scholarship and publish thought-provoking works of analysis in the fields of leadership and ethics, with special attention to their application to the military; to further CNO initiatives in leadership and ethics; to help educate Naval War College students; and to help inform the joint force. The Naval War College and the Naval War College Press thank the Naval War College Foundation and the Alletta Morris McBean Charitable Trust for their generous support.

The views expressed in the works of the Van Beuren series are those of the authors and do not necessarily reflect the opinions of the Naval War College or the Department of the Navy.

Correspondence concerning the Van Beuren series may be addressed to the Director of the Naval War College Press. To request additional copies, back copies, or subscriptions to the series, please either write the President (Code 32S), Naval War College, 686 Cushing Road, Newport, RI 02841-1207, or contact the Press staff at the telephone, fax, or e-mail addresses given.

CONTENTS

Foreword   iii

INTRODUCTION   1

THE U.S. NAVY'S AFRICAN AMERICAN ADMIRALS   7
  Vice Admiral Samuel L. Gravely Jr.   7
  Rear Admiral Gerald E. Thomas   12
  Rear Admiral Louis Williams   14
  Rear Admiral Wendell Norman Johnson   16
  Rear Admiral Benjamin T. Hacker   19
  Rear Admiral Robert Lee Toney   21
  Rear Admiral William E. Powell Jr.   24
  Vice Admiral Walter Davis   26
  Rear Admiral Macea E. Fussell   29
  Rear Admiral Mack Gaston   31
  Admiral Joseph Paul Reason   33
  Rear Admiral James A. Johnson   37
  Rear Admiral Larry L. Poe   40
  Vice Admiral Edward Moore Jr.   43
  Vice Admiral David L. Brewer III   47
  Rear Admiral Osie V. Combs   52
  Rear Admiral Gene Kendall   54
  Vice Admiral Adam M. Robinson Jr.   57
  Rear Admiral Lillian E. Fishburne   60
  Rear Admiral Willie C. Marsh   63
  Rear Admiral Vinson E. Smith   66
  Rear Admiral Reubin B. Bookert   68
  Rear Admiral Barry C. Black   70
  Vice Admiral Derwood Curtis   73
  Rear Admiral Julius S. Caesar   78
  Vice Admiral Anthony L. Winns   81
  Rear Admiral Victor G. Guillory   85
  Rear Admiral Arthur J. Johnson   88

Rear Admiral Earl L. Gay   90
Rear Admiral Kelvin N. Dixon   93
Rear Admiral Sinclair Harris   96
Rear Admiral Norman R. Hayes   100
Rear Admiral Vincent L. Griffith   103
Admiral Michelle Howard   106
Rear Admiral Charles K. Carodine   110
Rear Admiral Kevin D. Scott   113
Rear Admiral John W. Smith Jr.   116
Rear Admiral Jesse A. Wilson Jr.   119
Rear Admiral James W. Crawford III   122
Rear Admiral Annie B. Andrews   125
Rear Admiral Fernandez Ponds   128
Rear Admiral Dwight D. Shepherd   133
Rear Admiral Willie L. Metts   136
Rear Admiral Eric C. Young   139
Rear Admiral Stephen C. Evans   143
Rear Admiral Alvin Holsey   147

THE U.S. NAVY'S CENTENNIAL SEVEN   **150**
Captain C. A. 'Pete' Tzomes   151
Rear Admiral Anthony Watson   153
Dr. William F. Bundy   155
Vice Admiral Melvin G. Williams Jr.   159
Admiral Cecil D. Haney   164
Vice Admiral Bruce E. Grooms   167
Captain Joseph P. Peterson   171

SPECIAL RECOGNITION: THE HEART OF COMMAND AND
SENIOR LEADERSHIP   **173**
Rear Admiral Lawrence C. Chambers   173
The Honorable B. J. "Buddie" Penn   179

Conclusion   **183**

Acronyms and Abbreviations   **184**

African American Admirals Commissioning and Promotion Data **187**

About the Author   **190**

Notes   **191**

FOREWORD

In 1976, while serving in the Gold Crew of USS *Sam Houston,* I met then-Vice Adm. Samuel L. Gravely Jr., Commander Third Fleet. Admiral Gravely reached out to African American Navy officers in Pearl Harbor to offer an opportunity to meet him. I would later sit with Admiral Gravely at National Naval Officers Association (NNOA) conferences and in mentoring sessions with other African American officers. We sought his advice and gained the benefit of his views on success, such as the following:

> Success in life is the result of several factors. My formula is simply education plus motivation plus perseverance. Education is paramount. Motivation: one must decide what he [or she] wants to do in life, how best to get there, and proceed relentlessly toward that goal. Perseverance: the ability to steadfastly proceed to your goal despite all obstacles. It is the ability to overcome.

> One byproduct of my success is a role that has been thrust upon me: to serve as an inspiration for others coming along. I accept that role as graciously as I can, because there are people out there who feel I am sort of a role model.
>   Vice Adm. Samuel L. Gravely Jr. and Paul Stillwell, with Alma Gravely, *Trailblazer: The U.S. Navy's First Black Admiral,* p. 237.

In those days, we could easily count and individually meet the small but growing number of African American Navy captains and the few flag officers who had followed Admiral Gravely into the senior leadership ranks of the Navy and Marine Corps. It was not unusual to have all the African American Navy admirals, Marine Corps generals, and potential flag officers in a single room at NNOA conferences. There was camaraderie among us and an ardent mentoring environment that flowed down from admirals and generals to the newest ensigns and lieutenants.

There was also the prevailing atmosphere in those NNOA gatherings that our careers and successes were tied together with recruiting, retaining, and promoting African American sea service officers, supporting professional development, and building excellence. We fought for the notion that the Navy and Marine Corps should have 6 percent African American officers and about 18 percent African American enlisted sailors and Marines.

We had just begun to experience the changes in the Navy that became possible in the aftermath of Adm. Elmo Zumwalt's Z-Gram 66. As I look back on my experience in the Navy before and after Z-Gram 66, I am grateful for the courage that Admiral Zumwalt and Secretary of the Navy John Chafee demonstrated in addressing racial discrimination in the Navy. I gained personally from the adoption of equal opportunity in the Navy that was engendered by Z-66 and Secretary Chafee's ALNAV 51.[1]

To grasp fully the significance of the life stories in this book, Z-Gram 66, excerpted below, should be read in its entirety. Without its issuance or some equivalent courageous act to advance equal opportunity, the flag officers and other leaders featured in this record of professional accomplishment would not have been able to serve, and the line of officers would have been formed by some later succession of African Americans. In part, Admiral Zumwalt wrote as follows:

CNO {Z-66} 172054Z Dec 70
Equal Opportunity in the Navy

The purpose of this NAVOP is to express my wholehearted support of the policies on equal opportunity strongly reaffirmed by the Secretary of the Navy in ALNAV 51, to express my general guidance for implementation of these policies, and to direct implementation of a few of the actions we can take immediately.

[W]hat struck me more than anything else was the depth of feeling of our black personnel that there is significant discrimination in the Navy. Prior to these meetings, I sincerely believed that I was philosophically prepared to understand the problems of our black Navymen and their families, and until we discussed them at length, I did not realize the extent and deep significance of many of these matters.[2]

Vice Admiral Gravely's biography is recorded elsewhere (including in *Trailblazer,* referenced above [Naval Institute Press, 2010]). In this volume, Lt. Cdr. Robert Crosby offers a brief version of that biography, along with similar biographies of those African American Navy officers who followed Gravely into historic and senior leadership roles in the Navy.

Navy officers serve in demanding and usually dangerous environments, where they assume ultimate accountability for the successes and failures of their ships and commands. These accounts of the early lives, Navy appointments, and career accomplishments of the African American officers who followed in the trail that Vice Admiral Gravely blazed are offered to document the determination demonstrated and the successes achieved, under the often trying circumstances of bias encountered and obstacles that had to be overcome that the admiral mentioned in his formula for success.

Lieutenant Commander Crosby undertook this research project to answer lingering doubts that surround the implementation of equal opportunity policies instituted to eliminate discrimination and offer opportunities to all. Too often, we hear that individuals who benefit from such policies are not qualified or equal to the task. The biographies that Crosby has gathered document the leadership expected of and the successes achieved by all commissioned officers who rise to flag rank in the Navy. The fact that each of the African American officers who shared his or her story was highly successful validates that success is a matter of education, motivation, and perseverance—just as Admiral Gravely often shared in his mentoring sessions.

Our U.S. Navy has become a force that reflects the diverse citizenry of the United States that we in the armed forces protect and defend. As we together stand guard to defend the freedoms we embrace now and maintain them into the future, this is only just and right.

This first installment in the Van Beuren Leadership and Ethics series was undertaken originally as a Naval War College advanced research project within the Vice Adm. Samuel L. Gravely Jr. Naval Warfare Research Group.

Professor William F. Bundy, PhD
Director, the Gravely Group

INTRODUCTION

> [Vice Admiral] Gravely was an inspiration, not only to African
> Americans but to all naval officers aspiring to be the best that they
> can be. To this day, I think he is still an inspiration to us all, just an
> absolutely wonderful officer, gentleman, and a Christian. He strived
> to mentor and promote excellence in all junior officers, without
> regard to race or gender.
>
> Rear Adm. Anthony Winns, quoted in Ben L. Walton,
Great Black War Fighters: Profiles in Service

Samuel L. Gravely Jr. was a man of many firsts in African American history:

- Commanding a U.S. Navy warship
- Commanding an American warship under combat conditions (since the Civil War)
- Becoming an admiral in the U.S. Navy
- Commanding a U.S. fleet

And the list goes on. Gravely's accomplishments—the result of his perseverance, professionalism, and perpetual optimism—directly and indirectly paved the way for numerous Navy officers, and they continue to provide valuable lessons for us all.[3]

Gravely enlisted in the Navy on September 15, 1942, five months after the Navy altered its policy to allow African Americans to serve beyond the messman rating.[4] Over the course of his long career, Gravely made significant contributions to modern naval warfare. His crowning professional achievement was the direct responsibility he exercised to ensure that all Navy commands had access to satellite communications. While attached to the Satellite Communications Command, Gravely conceptualized and initiated a worldwide restructuring of shore communications facilities, resources, and responsibilities that proved very effective in an era of dwindling resources.[5]

Vice Admiral Gravely's distinguished career in the Navy continued a legacy derived from many other African Americans who significantly contributed to the defense of the nation, dating back to the American Revolution. They demonstrated remarkable courage and displayed a loyalty toward their country that surpassed their personal desires for freedom. For example, Prince Estabrook, a slave and a Massachusetts militiaman, stood with his musket on Lexington Green in April 1775 during America's "first glorious morning." Prince Whippleman, a slave from New Hampshire, provided dedicated service to George Washington as an oarsman in the boat in which Washington crossed the frigid Delaware River to make his Christmas Eve attack on the British in 1776. Nero Hawley, a Connecticut slave, was one of the starving and poorly dressed patriots who accompanied Washington during the terrible winter of 1777–78 at Valley Forge. Barzillai Lew, a free Massachusetts coppersmith, fifer, and drummer, uplifted and encouraged American spirits by playing "Yankee Doodle" at the battle of Bunker Hill. During the Civil War, Robert Smalls, a mulatto slave, freed himself and his family from slavery in 1862 by capturing the Confederate transport ship CSS *Planter* and sailing it to freedom beyond the federal blockade. It was Captain Robert Small's daring, courage, and creativity that encouraged Abraham Lincoln to accept African American soldiers into the Union Army. In reference to African Americans' wartime service in general, Harriet Beecher Stowe may have captured their contributions best in her preface to William Cooper Nell's *Colored Patriots of the American Revolution:* "We are to reflect upon them as far more magnanimous because rendered to a nation, which did not acknowledge them as citizens and equals . . . but for a land which had enslaved them and whose laws, even in freedom, more often oppressed than protected. Bravery under such circumstances has a peculiar beauty and merit."[6]

Gravely joined the Navy in hopes of learning a practical trade and exploring new horizons.[7] Little did he know that he would become a trailblazer who would open doors for thousands of other African American officers. This is his enduring legacy.[8] Vice Admiral Gravely always remembered those on whose shoulders he stood and was driven to inspire others. He would tell young people: "Success in life is the result of several factors. My formula is simply education plus motivation plus perseverance. Education is paramount. Motivation: one must decide what he wants to do in life and how best to get there, and proceed relentlessly toward that goal. Perseverance: The ability to steadfastly proceed to your goal despite all obstacles. It is the ability to overcome."[9]

Vice Admiral Gravely's career in the Navy spanned thirty-five years. After his initial enlistment in 1942, he was released from active duty in 1946, but remained in the Naval Reserve. He returned to civilian life to complete his bachelor's degree in history. Gravely was recalled to active duty in 1949 as part of the Navy's response to President Harry Truman's executive order 9981 to desegregate the armed services. Gravely's initial assignment was to recruit African Americans in the Washington, DC, area. His last tour of duty, before retiring in August 1980, was as director of the Defense Communications Agency.

Gravely's influence brought diversity to the Navy that led to intellectual creativity in its thought and leadership that benefited all. This paper focuses on the background and the operational, policy, and technical contributions of Vice Adm. Samuel L. Gravely and his legacy of African American flag officers. Like Gravely, the majority of his successors overcame social, economic, and workplace isolation to achieve success and help others while boosting national defense. Their efforts and experiences serve to inspire the current generation of officers to strive to personify innovative leadership and dedication to the Navy and the nation, and will continue to inspire future generations.

What follows is a collection of individual accounts of the career accomplishments of Vice Admiral Gravely's successors. These accounts reveal the common themes of their life stories: being reared in humble surroundings; receiving strong family influences; and having a desire—in some cases feeling a duty—to achieve, regardless of institutional and personal obstacles. They also share a heritage derived from both their ancestry and the influence of servant leaders in the military who encouraged them to "stick it out." Each of these leaders was often the only African American assigned to his or her submarine, surface ship, or aircraft squadron. For these patriots, failure was not an option. They carried with them not only their personal determination to succeed, but the possible opportunities for others who would follow in their paths as well.

Some of Vice Admiral Gravely's successors experienced severe workplace isolation and reached the verge of resigning from the armed services, but were saved by the intervention of a mentor. This leads to another theme of this research: for every individual who sought to cause professional harm to African American officers, there were three or four others ready and willing to assist. While the lack of mentors was common for most of the early successors to Gravely, later successors enjoyed an abundance of support and assistance from commanding officers and senior leaders who became increasingly impressed with their attitude and work ethic and less concerned about their ethnicity.

The members of Vice Admiral Gravely's cadre of trailblazing patriots continue to serve our nation in the military or in other professional capacities. Collectively they continue to motivate the nation's young people and its future leaders. They not only mentor young military professionals, but serve their greater communities by volunteering at local schools and in other public venues. They understand the value of mentoring; several cite mentoring as the saving grace for themselves personally and professionally. They also understand the risks associated with failing to guide and mentor those who follow in their footsteps. According to the National Mentoring Partnership:

- Mentors help improve a young person's self-esteem.[10]
- Youth who meet regularly with their mentors are 46 percent less likely than their peers to start using illegal drugs and 27 percent less likely to start drinking.[11]
- About 40 percent of a teenager's waking hours are spent without companionship or supervision. Mentors provide teens with a valuable place to spend free time.[12]
- Mentors teach young people how to relate well to all kinds of people and help them strengthen communication skills.[13]

Children in underserved communities typically are afforded fewer opportunities, in environments less forgiving of their mistakes compared to other communities in the United States. That is why mentoring is also supported by President Obama's My Brother's Keeper initiative. Our cadre of trailblazers has answered this call to duty time and time again by making mentoring a priority.

The Navy officers interviewed for this research have contributed significantly to national defense by leading various military and maritime operations, including but not limited to Operations FREQUENT WIND, DESERT STORM, DESERT SHIELD, IRAQI FREEDOM, and ENDURING FREEDOM. They also led and contributed significantly to a host of Cold War operations, amphibious operations, Tomahawk employment engagements, defense communications support, strategic asset management, nuclear strategic force employment, cyber warfare, technology acquisition, expeditionary warfare employment, and other operations and forward deployments to hotspots around the world. Understanding how they persevered through turbulent social, economic, and military pressures will provide insight to and compelling inspiration for our aspiring youth and current and future naval leaders.

African-American admirals, active duty and retired, in attendance at the ceremony at which USS *Gravely* (DDG 107) was commissioned into active service in the United States Navy.

Photo courtesy of Dr. William F. Bundy

Gathering the Details of Navy History

Surprisingly, little written information exists about the specific operational, policy, and technical contributions that Vice Admiral Gravely and other African American flag officers have made in the Navy. Most of the information about these accomplishments included herein is provided via oral histories or interviews (most of each Background section) and military award citations (most of each Significant Contributions section).

A note about documentation: a single citation at the end of any section may cover an entire multi-paragraph section. Where award citations are used, a section of text may consist of excerpts from citations, paraphrased versions, or both. The full text of the originals is available online via the Naval War College website; however, citations were not necessarily available to cover all stages of every officer's career. Because award citations and other records of military affairs make use of numerous abbreviations and acronyms, explanations of the ones most commonly used in this work are gathered in a list at the back for reference, rather than explaining them repetitively in the text. No records of award citations for Vice Admiral Gravely are available before he reached the rank of commander; therefore, limited information is available about his accomplishments during his junior-officer years.

This first installment in the Van Beuren series on leadership and ethics began as a Naval War College advanced graduate research project. Research began with Vice Admiral Gravely, then moved on to gathering a comprehensive list of African American admirals who have served in the U.S. Navy. Research on individuals followed, by locating living admirals and conducting interviews, either by telephone or in person. In each case, the draft of interview results was presented to the officer interviewed for correction and amendment. What follows are the personal accounts of African American Navy officers who shared their stories and accomplishments. To this point, over fifty officers have attained the rank of admiral in the U.S. Navy, and most have been interviewed for this research, along with Dr. William F. Bundy, Captain Joe Peterson, Captain Pete Tzomes, and the Honorable B. J. "Buddie" Penn. Dr. Bundy is a retired commander and the director of the Vice Admiral Samuel L. Gravely Jr. Naval Warfare Research Group at the U.S. Naval War College. Captain Peterson lives in Atlanta, Georgia, having recently retired from a position supporting the Submarine Division at the Naval Sea Systems Command. Captain Tzomes, the first African American submarine commanding officer, works in the nuclear power industry. The Honorable Mr. Penn, the only African American to serve as acting Secretary of the Navy, remains very involved in strategic naval affairs. Dr. Bundy, Captain Peterson, and Captain Tzomes are three of the Centennial Seven submarine skippers (explained in more detail later).

A note on admirals: The rank of rear admiral in the U.S. Navy has two divisions, upper (senior) and lower (junior). An upper-half rear admiral is designated O-8, wears two stars on his or her uniform, and receives a higher rate of pay than a lower-half counterpart (designated O-7, wearing one star). Rear admirals assist vice admirals (O-9), who wear three stars and are one rank above an upper-half rear admiral.[14] Four-star admirals (O-10) are properly called simply "admiral," but are sometimes referred to as "full admiral" to avoid confusion and distinguish them from flag officers of lower ranks. Each grade's command flag contains a corresponding number of stars on a blue background.

In 1971, Samuel L. Gravely Jr. became the first African American to be promoted to the rank of rear admiral. Since that time, over fifty African Americans have become rear admirals.[15] Rear Admiral Gerald E. Thomas, the second African American to attain that rank in the U.S. Navy, achieved the distinction in 1975.

Officer promotions in the U.S. Navy are linked to progressive career assignments that build competency in wider responsibilities of command. Each warfare and unrestricted line community has a fairly clear path to promotion to the highest levels in the Navy. Early on, commanders who were biased would limit opportunities for African Americans to excel in their roles or offer faint praise as a means to undermine the efforts of otherwise competent and high-performing officers to advance. African American officers began to become three- and four-star admirals as the Navy began to embrace diversity in the form of a number of initiatives that enabled rear admirals to serve successfully in critical assignments. As the number of African American rear admirals increased and the visibility of that cadre of exceptionally talented officers became more prominent, it was inevitable that African American officers would accede to the "right" assignments and ultimately be promoted to vice admiral and then full admiral. J. Paul Reason was the first African American Navy officer promoted to the rank of admiral.

Here are the stories of Vice Admiral Samuel L. Gravely Jr. and the U.S. Navy trailblazers who followed in his footsteps.

THE U.S. NAVY'S AFRICAN AMERICAN ADMIRALS

Vice Admiral Samuel L. Gravely Jr.

Background

Vice Admiral Gravely's Navy career spanned from 1942 to 1980. The first African American Navy admiral pinned on his first star in 1971, thirty years after the Army named its first African American general and seventeen years after the newly created Air Force did so.[16] Gravely had been a pigeon fancier since he was twelve years old; he was quiet and soft-spoken, and did not enjoy the spotlight. On achieving the rank of admiral, he objected to conducting interviews with *Ebony* magazine and other publications, insisting that he only wanted to do his job, like any other sailor. According to his widow:

> Sammie loved the Navy but never thought he would make it to admiral status. He never did like all the publicity he got. He was quiet and was always determined to do his best in any situation. So many individuals played a role in helping him and it's because of good people—black, white, and any other color—that we made it. . . . I called him 'Sammy the Sailor,' and his motto was 'Sailors belong on ships and ships belong at sea.' We were married for fifty-eight years, and they were the best years of my life.[17]

Amid an environment of racism and inequality, Samuel Gravely rose through the ranks. His love for the Navy and the sea transcended the social inequalities he experienced in his day. These included workplace isolation, official Navy policy limitations, and insufficient housing while transferring between duty stations. A glimpse into his personal and professional life provides a new perspective into what it means to be an American.

Gravely came from modest roots, but he compensated with an intense work ethic. He was born in Richmond, Virginia, on June 4, 1922, to Samuel Sr. and Mary George Gravely. Gravely's parents were not formally educated, but they taught him and his four younger brothers and sisters a solid work ethic, discipline, and the drive always to perform to the best of their abilities in any situation. On one occasion, Samuel Jr. was offered an opportunity to sweep the sidewalk of Mr. Harrison, a drugstore owner, for a dime. When he completed the task, he went home to inform his parents of his newfound fortune. Gravely Sr. responded, "Son, I just got off the streetcar at the corner, and that place doesn't look like it's been swept to me. You give me that dime and we're going to walk back there and see if Mr. Harrison will let us do it again so I can show you how to do a proper job."[18]

Samuel Jr. would never forget that lesson. His father worked as a Pullman porter and a postal worker. His mother worked as a domestic for white families in the suburbs of Richmond. Owing to his mother's encouragement, he became the first African American to deliver newspapers for the *Richmond Times Dispatch*. Every summer she sent Samuel Jr. to summer school to advance his studies and keep him out of trouble. Because of her dedication and foresight, he graduated from high school at fifteen.[19]

Samuel Jr. experienced tragedy early on: when he was fifteen the mother who had been so very influential in his life died after a prolonged illness. A week after her death, his brother lost his right leg when a streetcar jumped the tracks and struck him. While his father worked to support them all, Samuel Jr. had to care for his brothers and sisters—feeding and dressing them and getting them off to school. This was his life until he graduated from high school.[20]

Then the Japanese attacked Pearl Harbor on December 7, 1941, and life drastically changed. Samuel Jr. understood that he would soon be drafted. His father proactively engaged with each service to see which would be a better fit for his son. Even though the military was segregated and blacks in the Navy were only allowed to be messmen, Samuel Jr. and his father eventually decided the Navy would be the best choice.[21]

Samuel Gravely Jr. served during a time of significant upheaval and disarray in the armed services. Five months prior to his enlistment, the Navy updated its recruiting policy concerning African Americans in the general ratings. According to Dennis Denmark Nelson in *The Integration of the Negro into the Navy:*

> On April 7, 1942, the Navy announced that it had relaxed its traditional policy of recruiting Negro men as messmen only, and effective June 1, would accept Negro volunteers in the Navy proper, in the Coast Guard, and in the Marine Corps, as seamen and in other capacities. These volunteers, the Navy made clear, would receive basic and advanced training in segregated units, and would be limited in assignment to shore installations and harbor craft. Negroes in general service ratings would not be billeted in seagoing vessels, but would be used principally in construction battalions under the Bureau of Yards and Docks, in supply depots, ordnance stations, and yard (harbor) craft. White petty officers were to be in command of the Negro units until Negro petty officers would be trained. There would be no Negro commissioned officers at all. The new policy was termed an "experiment."[22]

The first African American U.S. Navy officers. Photographed 17 March 1944.

Official U.S. Navy photograph, now in the collections of the National Archives

As World War II went on, it forced the Navy to reevaluate further its policies toward sailors of color. Many of its existing junior officers were exhausted from warfare, and the Navy needed to recruit astute individuals as their replacements. Thus started the V12 College Training Program. This program screened selected individuals for college placement and ultimately a commission in the Navy. Then a fireman apprentice, Gravely was directed by his division officer to apply. His training began at the University of California, followed by Pre-Midshipman School; and on December 14, 1944, he became the first African American to be commissioned from NROTC.[23]

Looking back at the age of ninety-two, Gravely's widow Alma observed, "It was hard on my husband in those days; for instance, as a young lieutenant in Miami, Florida, he was arrested for impersonating an officer."[24] However, Gravely not only survived but thrived. Over the next thirty-plus years, Gravely continued to break barriers and notched several "firsts" for the Navy, including being the first African American to enroll at the Naval War College, the first African American to command a U.S. Navy ship (USS *Theodore E. Chandler*), the first African American to command an American warship under combat conditions since the Civil War (USS *Taussig*), the first African American to command a major naval warship (USS *Jouett*), the first African American to become an admiral, the first African American to rise to the rank of vice admiral, and the first African American to command a U.S. fleet (Third Fleet).[25]

Significant Operational, Policy, and Technical Contributions

USS Taussig (DD 746)

As CO of *Taussig* during active combat operations, Gravely and his crew provided significant gunfire support to friendly ground forces in the Republic of South Vietnam. By exercising astute leadership, amazing innovation, and personal skill, Commander Gravely consistently supported U.S. and allied forces with extremely accurate and rapid naval gunfire in both coastal and inland waters. In another example of his courage and creativity under fire, he directed *Taussig*'s six-gun batteries with keen accuracy in support of troops of four nations on numerous occasions. This resulted in the destruction of six enemy defense structures and one supply area. On receiving an urgent request for supplemental gunfire support, his highly trained and efficient crew effortlessly regained the optimal firing position, destroyed fourteen enemy structures, and contributed significantly to several follow-on explosions of enemy constructions.[26]

Navy Satellite Communications Program

As the Navy's satellite communications program coordinator in April 1970, Captain Gravely was responsible for a Navy-wide effort to obtain satellite communications for naval forces of all echelons. This period was characterized by a critical shortage of resources and austere funding; however, Captain Gravely's innovative character was exceptionally effective in maintaining Navy visibility in the Defense Satellite Communications System while assuring optimum economy of Navy funds and manpower. Captain Gravely creatively managed a development-assistance project that demonstrated the feasibility and advantages of satellite communications for naval forces. His untiring efforts to ensure the Navy possessed reliable, real-time, secure communications for C2 significantly contributed to Navy and DoD global leadership in defense communications.[27]

Vice Adm. Samuel L. Gravely Jr.
Naval History and Heritage Command photograph.

Director, Naval Communications Division

In this position, Rear Admiral Gravely implemented the Fleet Satellite Communications Program and introduced the Consolidated Fleet Command Support Center, the Secure Imagery Transmission System, and the Ship-Shore-Ship Data Link. He conceptualized and initiated a worldwide restructuring of shore communications facilities, resources, and responsibilities, which proved very effective in an era of dwindling resources.[28]

Commander, Third Fleet

Vice Admiral Gravely sought innovative ways to maximize resources and training opportunities. Under his leadership, ASW warfare seminars were instituted in San Diego and Hawaii, which brought the entire ASW community together as a cohesive group. He initiated major programs, including the deployment of destroyer squadrons and carriers as integral units and the dedication of an SSN to accompany each deploying carrier task group to maximize ASW training en route.[29]

Director, Defense Communications Agency

Vice Admiral Gravely was the director of the DCA, now the Defense Information Systems Agency, from September 1978 to July 1980. Under his leadership, the DCA covered the entire spectrum of defense communications, coordinating all satellite communications to prevent duplication. Vice Admiral Gravely's leadership and direction laid the groundwork for the launch of the Defense Systems Communication Satellites III (DSCS-III) in 1982.[30] The DSCS-III was a third-generation, multipurpose, military communications satellite.[31] It provided the backbone for all DoD satellite capabilities and nuclear-hardened, antijam, high-data-rate, and long-haul communications across the globe. Fourteen DSCS-III satellites were launched from the early 1980s to 2003. Vice Admiral Gravely contributed significantly to this technological development for DoD. He also made lasting contributions to improving our nation's defense posture in the field of command, control, and communications. His direct leadership and creativity kept the DCA at the forefront of technology, while maintaining the highest level of communication support to national command authorities.[32]

Rear Admiral Gerald E. Thomas

United States Naval Institute

Background

Gerald E. Thomas was born in 1929 in Natick, Massachusetts, to Walter and Leila Thomas. He was commissioned via the Harvard University NROTC unit in 1951, the first African American commissioned through that accession program.

Thomas became the second African American appointed to the rank of rear admiral in the U.S. Navy, in November 1974. In 1981, President Reagan appointed him ambassador extraordinary and minister plenipotentiary to Guyana, and in 1983 to Kenya.[33]

Significant Operational, Policy, and Technical Contributions

Commanding Officer, USS Bausell *(DD 845)*

Commander Thomas' ship provided outstanding support to the task group commander by providing accurate and excellent gunfire that destroyed several coastal-defense sites, a transshipment point, and a choke point. During Operation Sea Dragon, which interdicted all North Vietnamese supply lines going into South Vietnam, his ship performed with tireless professionalism and successfully completed every mission assigned.[34]

Commanding Officer, Prairie View A&M University NROTC Unit

Commander Thomas demonstrated exceptional administrative and leadership ability by ensuring the rapid maturation of the two-year-old program at Prairie View. His inspirational guidance enabled the university to attain a competitive status and compete with other NROTC units across the country. His ability was exemplified when he established an effective flight indoctrination program at minimum cost to the school. It is largely because of his efforts that Prairie View has produced more African American flag officers than any other institution in the country, with the exception of USNA.[35]

Commander, Training Command, U.S. Pacific Fleet

While in this position, Rear Admiral Thomas dramatically increased the scope of training and functional services provided to the fleet, while simultaneously increasing the quality of training. His direct efforts transformed the fleet, preparing it for any contingency tasking. Under his guidance, two major projects were conceived to improve the tactical readiness of the Pacific Fleet: the Tactical Training Group Pacific and the Commander Training Command. These two projects provided a marked improvement in the tactical skills and knowledge of battle group staffs, which resulted in significantly enhanced Pacific Fleet battle readiness.[36]

Rear Admiral Louis Williams

United States Naval Institute

Background

Louis Williams grew up in a poor family from Ypsilanti, Michigan. He eventually made his way to San Francisco to study architectural engineering in college.

Williams loved flying, which prompted him to enlist in the Navy. In the late 1950s, Williams broke the color barrier, becoming the first black instructor at Naval Air Station Pensacola, the cradle of Navy aviation. He would later fly reconnaissance missions throughout the Vietnam War. As a rear admiral in the early 1980s, he oversaw scientific projects in Antarctica. His career concluded with a high-ranking NATO position in Portugal.

Williams never viewed himself as a racial trailblazer. Said his wife, Faye Williams, "Race was never a big issue with him. He believed you can do whatever you wanted to do if you put forth the effort. He made others believe that, too." She added, "It was the nature of the man to love challenges."[37]

Significant Operational, Policy, and Technical Contributions

Antisubmarine Squadron 23

While at this command, Lieutenant Commander Williams was commended for working under an intense operational tempo with the Seventh Fleet, involving an extraordinary number of days at sea and around-the-clock flying. The engagements included protracted and highly skilled intelligence-producing surveillance of Soviet submarines in the Philippine Sea, direct support of combat strikes by TF 77 against North Vietnam, and anti-infiltration patrols as part of Operation MARKET TIME OFF THE COAST OF SOUTH VIETNAM. Most of these operations required countless hours in the air amid hostile forces, and their success was a testament to Lieutenant Commander Williams' professional skill and inspirational leadership.[38]

Commanding Officer, Naval Air Station Agana, Guam, and Refugee Airlift Coordinator

During a period of arduous effort, Captain Williams' inspirational leadership ensured success in the urgent mission to position U.S. forces and use them to support and process on Guam more than 110,000 refugees being evacuated from Southeast Asia. He was directly responsible for planning and directing all aspects of refugee arrival to and processing on the island. His tact and sensitivity to the refugees were instrumental to their welfare. His foresight and planning led to the efficient and safe manner in which more than 35,000 refugees were flown in more than 200 military aircraft.[39]

Rear Admiral Wendell Norman Johnson

Background

Wendell Norman Johnson, the son of immigrants from Barbados, was reared in Roxbury, Boston, Massachusetts. His father, who had been a certified public accountant in Barbados, eventually became a merchant mariner. His mother was an elevator operator.

Even at a young age, Wendell was very focused. In the early 1950s, while he was completing his application to attend the Boston Latin School, he noticed another student staring at him intently. The other boy finally asked, "Darky, can I borrow a pencil, please?" Wendell handed the boy a pencil—and never once thought to confront him about the term of address. When asked later why he did not, he replied, "The matter was to get into Latin School, not to jump up and take offense." He eventually did get into the school. After graduating, he attended the New England School of Pharmacy.

Admiral Johnson was very patriotic, and he enjoyed sailing with his father on various waterways. Consequently, when he was drafted by the Army in 1955, he chose to enlist in the Navy. Encountering racism was commonplace in the country during the 1960s, but he did not allow that to deter him from serving his country proudly. He later recalled a story that had been published in *The Boston University Alumni Magazine.* A waiter refused to serve him in a restaurant near his military base:

> I said to him, "Take a look around this place—it looks to me like they're all sailors, and if you refuse to serve me I'll go back to the base and say you're not serving

sailors." He also recalled, "Most blacks in the Navy were in service functions when I joined, such as laundrymen, cooks, and stewards . . . but as the Navy realized we had something more to offer, blacks were allowed to attend school and earn some of the critical ratings, such as sonarman, radioman, and machinist. The black officers I knew and some of the fellows coming out of the Naval Academy were getting better assignments. But it was a hard nut to crack when you think of the history of the U.S. Navy and how long it was truly segregated.

Johnson encountered additional experiences of this type in the military, but by the early 1970s he was in Washington, DC, assisting Admiral Elmo R. Zumwalt Jr. on diversity programs for the Navy. He was one of the founding fathers of the BOOST initiative— which gave this author the educational uplift to become a nuclear submarine officer. Johnson's trailblazing experiences and the work he put into improving diversity in the Navy helped countless other minority officers rise to the executive level in the naval service. His life left a lasting legacy not only on the Navy, but on the nation as a whole.[40]

Significant Operational, Policy, and Technical Contributions

Weapons Officer, USS Ingraham *(DD 694)*

Lieutenant Commander Johnson demonstrated exceptional professional competency and leadership while orchestrating the firing of over 1,800 rounds in support of eleven naval gunfire support missions. As gunnery officer, he ensured that every detailed call for fire was delivered with pinpoint accuracy and without delay. He persevered through long and tedious hours of general quarters, succeeding in motivating his men to the point of peak efficiency. His keen technical knowledge afforded him the opportunity to resolve all fire-control problems, including fire-control authority and accuracy, prior to executing every single mission.[41]

Head, Minority Recruiting Effort, Bureau of Naval Personnel

While serving as head of the Navy's effort to recruit minorities for the services, Lieutenant Commander Johnson displayed superior leadership and sensitivity to interpersonal relationships that allowed him to respond extremely effectively in matters of potential interracial tension in the Navy. He astutely developed and executed a plan to increase diversity in the naval service; he visited several HBCUs to showcase the Navy and the opportunities it offered. He developed the Minority Recruiting Guide and was a founding father of the BOOST program, which provided selected minorities the opportunity to become better educated so they could compete for Navy scholarships. Because of his direct efforts during his tenure, minority officer strength doubled in the Navy and minority enlisted strength reversed a downward trend as well.[42]

Special Assistant to the Chief of Naval Personnel for Equal Opportunity Matters

Commander Johnson innovatively developed a wide spectrum of specific actions and initiatives during the early 1970s, a turbulent period for race relations in the Navy. He demonstrated exceptional perception, imagination, and foresight in identifying problem areas and recommending courses of action to resolve them. Because of his superb judgment and outstanding professional skills in analyzing courses of actions and articulating sound recommendations for the direction and control of the Navy Race Relations and Human Goals Program, countless minority officers were given the opportunity to serve and thrive in the Navy.[43]

Commanding Officer, USS Jason (AR 8)

Captain Johnson demonstrated his extreme competence and imaginative and resourceful leadership by molding and directing his command to become the most productive and respected maintenance ship in the Pacific Fleet. His professionalism in providing repair service in the eastern Pacific made *Jason* the most sought-after repair ship on the waterfront. His broad knowledge of ship repair was the catalyst behind the ship receiving the prestigious battle efficiency "E," as well as six departmental excellence awards.

Johnson's concern for sailors and his efforts in promoting pride and professionalism contributed to an exceptional personnel program, resulting in *Jason* being awarded the coveted Silver Anchor Award for leading the force in retention.[44]

Director, Joint and Operational Logistics Plans and Programs Division

Rear Admiral Johnson's direction and leadership brought several planning and programming initiatives to fruition. He initiated the first Baseline Area Appraisal and Strategic Logistics Appraisal, which examined the Navy's ability to support the Maritime Strategy logistically. This program identified strengths and limitations of the Navy logistics system. His foresight in planning was the catalyst behind the development of guidance to clarify the assignment of functions and responsibilities within the Navy logistics system. This effort increased the logistics system's effectiveness, and his efforts resulted in vastly improved readiness and sustainability for the Navy that lasted decades.[45]

Rear Admiral Benjamin T. Hacker

Background

Benjamin Thurman Hacker was born in Washington, DC, on September 19, 1935. After completing high school, mostly in Daytona Beach, Florida, he attended the University of Dayton and Wittenberg University, both in Ohio. He graduated in June 1957 with a bachelor's degree in science and joined the Navy soon thereafter.

After completing AOCS at Pensacola, Florida, Hacker was commissioned an ensign in September 1958. He was designated a naval flight officer in June 1960. In March 1960, he was promoted to lieutenant (junior grade), and in October 1962 to lieutenant. He served with Patrol Squadron 10 and Patrol Squadron 21 from 1960 to 1963. In 1963, he reported to the Naval Postgraduate School in Monterey, California, where he completed the engineering science curriculum.

In 1972, he established the NROTC unit at Florida A&M University in Tallahassee, and served as the unit's first professor of naval science and CO. In May 1986, he was awarded an honorary degree by George Washington University, Washington, DC. Rear Admiral Hacker became commander, NTC San Diego in August 1986, and thereafter commander, Naval Base San Diego.[46]

Significant Operational, Policy, and Technical Contributions

Patrol Squadron 21

Lieutenant Hacker was commended for meritorious performance of flight operations in support of the U.S. quarantine of Cuba from October 25, 1962, to December 3, 1962, while attached to Fleet Air Wing 3. When tasked, Hacker's squadron expertly and quickly deployed to advanced bases in the Atlantic Ocean and conducted sustained, long-range surveillance. Despite hazardous weather, all flights arrived on time. He displayed an aggressive spirit, outstanding readiness for combat, and technical competence. He, along with other members of the squadron, worked diligently and acquired operational intelligence vital to the national interest.[47]

Commanding Officer, Naval Air Station Brunswick, Maine

In this capacity, Captain Hacker's leadership empowered the air station to achieve a production rate of 99.9 percent, the highest of any COMNAVAIRLANT activity. He significantly decreased the backlog of essential, funded maintenance and repair projects; several housing projects were accomplished, including major military construction projects funded by NATO; and he led an extraordinary command retention program.[48]

Commander, Fleet Air, Mediterranean; Maritime Reconnaissance and Surveillance Forces, Sixth Fleet; and Maritime Air Forces, Mediterranean

Rear Admiral Hacker exercised direct control over several shore commands and the Navy's largest fleet air reconnaissance squadron. Using astute geopolitical insight and anticipation, he forestalled problems and advanced numerous initiatives to improve fleet support. He led the establishment of the first vertical onboard delivery squadron in the Mediterranean.[49]

Commander, Naval Training Center, San Diego, California

Rear Admiral Hacker's dynamic leadership in and personal commitment to community affairs enhanced the Navy's image and placed the NTC in the spotlight. He created the Saturday Scholars program, the first of its kind in the western region of the country, to promote education and personal excellence. A powerful and dynamic speaker, he addressed equal opportunity issues and promoted equal opportunity in front of virtually every powerful and significant community group in San Diego.[50]

Rear Admiral Robert Lee Toney

Background

Robert Toney was born in Monroe, Louisiana. Eventually he was the second oldest of five siblings. During World War II his family moved to Oakland, California, where his father, who wanted to contribute to the war effort, worked for a company that made patrol boats for the Navy. In 1948, after the war was over, the family moved to Oroville, California, where his father was employed in the lumber business. Robert graduated from Oroville High School in 1952.

After finishing high school, Robert attended Chico State University. Initially, his family encouraged him to become a lawyer, and he even applied and was accepted to law school. However, his Chico State adviser urged him always to "keep more than one iron in the fire," and he also informed Toney that becoming an officer in the Navy would preclude him from being drafted. This caused Toney to apply for the Navy OCS located in Newport, Rhode Island. He received a letter from his draft board and a letter from OCS almost simultaneously; he chose the latter option. There were only three African American officer candidates in his class of 1,300.

While serving as XO of a vessel in Treasure Island, California, he was selected to work in the Bureau of Naval Personnel in Washington, DC, where his primary role was to increase the number of African American officers. (At this time, there were fewer than fifty African American officers in the entire Navy.) He and his team of three set out to visit each HBCU to inform the students about opportunities in the Navy. They also attended NAACP meetings and National Urban League meetings to understand African American officers better, so as to recruit them into the Navy more successfully.

Commander Toney and the members of his team also sought to mentor the new officers who were being recruited. While holed up in a hotel in Annapolis, Maryland, they devised a strategy and formed an organization called the National Naval Officers Association (NNOA). They established an overall purpose for the organization and structured it in regions. The NNOA still exists today, and the author has benefited from its mission of improving the operational readiness of the sea services by promoting a diverse force, as have countless others. CNO Admiral Elmo Zumwalt was instrumental in ensuring that NNOA got the initial funding and support it needed to make it through the organization's first tumultuous years of existence. Zumwalt provided Commander Toney with amazing leadership and mentorship in achieving his objective of increasing the number of African American officers in the Navy.

An interesting related note: one Saturday, Commander Toney was briefing Admiral Zumwalt on the issue of flag officers. Zumwalt asked, "Is there an African American you can recommend who is qualified to become an admiral?" Commander Toney and his team replied unanimously, "Captain Sam Gravely!" The following Monday, he and his team received word that Gravely was an admiral.[51]

Significant Operational, Policy, and Technical Contributions

Special Assistant to the Chief of Naval Personnel for Minority Recruiting

Commander Toney's efforts led to an increase in African American accessions from 5 percent in 1969 to almost 13 percent in 1972, a testament to his unparalleled critical analysis, inspirational leadership, and creative approach. Also during this time, total minority racial and ethnic group accessions increased from 8 percent to almost 17 percent. Although force reduction accounted for an unusual number of minority officer losses between 1969 and 1972, the number of African American officers on active duty rose from 450 to 660 and the total of minority officers from 592 to 958.

Toney's insightful vision enabled him to increase dramatically the incidence of MORE information and counseling team visits to more than sixty-nine accredited, pre-dominantly minority colleges and universities, as well as community and national-level organizations. This resulted in a discernible improvement in the Navy's image in minority communities. Commander Toney's professional acumen and competence contributed greatly to the effectiveness of minority recruiting efforts, including the establishment of enduring programs that have been responsible for thousands of minority officer accessions.[52]

Commander, Naval Base San Francisco, California

Rear Admiral Toney aggressively pursued actions that resulted in a better readiness posture and provided flexibility of operations throughout the eastern Pacific. He developed the logistics plans for Commander, Third Fleet's war-fighting strategy and promulgated the battle force commander's tactical logistics guide, which dramatically enhanced the Navy's ability to project sea power by streamlining the Pacific Fleet's combat logistics operations. He was an outstanding pillar for the Navy in the San Francisco Bay area, resolving critical issues that ranged from strategic homeporting to coordinating with civilian regulatory agencies on important environmental issues.[53]

Director, Logistics-Security Assistance, CINCPAC

Rear Admiral Toney spearheaded remarkable improvements in U.S. readiness and sustainability, as well as the war-fighting posture of friendly and allied military forces. He obtained the first wartime host-nation support agreements in the Pacific, with Korea.

When Iraq invaded Kuwait, Toney's management of logistics assets in the Pacific was exceptional. He opened a new era in cooperation between the U.S. and Japanese logistics communities. He created the first successful theater-wide humanitarian assistance program for excess property, and also developed CINCPAC's Concept of Logistics Support for Global War, which went into use worldwide.[54]

Rear Admiral William E. Powell Jr.

COMO (Sel.) WILLIAM E. POWELL, JR.
SC, USN
Director of
Supply Corps Personnel,
Naval Supply Systems Command
Washington, DC

Background

William E. Powell Jr. was born in Indianapolis, Indiana, in April 1936 and enlisted in the Navy in 1953. Powell completed recruit training at NTC Bainbridge, Maryland, and was selected to attend NAPS, Bainbridge, from which he received an appointment to USNA in 1955. Upon graduation in 1959, he attended Navy Supply Corps School in Athens, Georgia.[55]

In June 1966, Powell went to the Naval Supply Systems Command in Washington, where he was intimately involved in designing the Navy's future ships.[56] Throughout his career he routinely sought and received the most challenging assignments; these included an independent Supply Corps billet aboard USS *Nicholas* (DDE 449). He was rewarded with flag rank, becoming the first African American admiral in the Supply Corps. His pinnacle achievement was serving as CO of Naval Supply Center Norfolk, the world's largest supply center at the time.[57] In that role he modernized an already extremely productive organization with state-of-the-art tools to meet fleet demands even more rapidly.[58]

Significant Operational, Policy, and Technical Contributions

Assistant Director, Aviation Supply Programs

Captain Powell greatly enhanced naval aviation readiness by spearheading a review of USMC pack-up kit requirements, and channeled the program from operating concepts to problem resolution. He also successfully accelerated a new program that improved spares availability and aircraft materiel readiness aboard aircraft carriers.

Powell developed and presented briefs to the CNO, the Secretary of the Navy, congressional staff members, and other government officials to address logistics support for the F/A-18 program, Maritime Prepositioned Ships program, component repair, and aircraft materiel readiness overall.[59]

Commanding Officer, Naval Supply Depot, Subic Bay, the Philippines

Captain Powell expertly managed the operations, facilities, and personnel of the largest logistics complex in the Pacific fleet. His personal involvement and exceptional managerial ability were instrumental in providing vital and outstanding supply support services to Seventh Fleet units and shore activities. His inspirational efforts resulted in a substantial upgrade to the physical distribution capabilities of the depot, including the installation of a state-of-the-art gantry crane in the freight terminal department, implementation of an enhanced receiving concept in the material department, and a comprehensive inventory accuracy program that drove the annual gross monetary adjustment and warehouse refusal rates to impressively low levels.[60]

Commanding Officer, Naval Supply Center Norfolk

Admiral Powell maximized the center's operational capability to maintain the fleet in the highest possible readiness condition and sustainability. While operating with a budget decrease of over twenty-two million dollars combined with increased mission responsibilities, he exercised commendable managerial expertise, control, and innovation in balancing limited resources to meet or exceed financial and performance goals. He instituted a program that led to improved management information and load planning, as well as a cost center managerial approach that significantly contributed to his command's high standards of issue and receipt timeliness, inventory accuracy, material availability, and procurement competition. He was formally recognized by the Commander, Naval Supply System Command for directing the only naval supply center to exceed its business-plan level of physical distribution workload at less than the negotiated cost.[61]

Vice Admiral Walter Davis

Background

Walter Davis was raised in North Carolina and attended segregated schools, but rose to the highest levels of the Navy. While in high school, he was asked what he wanted to become as an adult, to which he replied, "An airline pilot." His math teacher, Mr. Togo West (later U.S. Secretary of Veterans Affairs), replied, "Have you ever seen any blacks as airline pilots? You should try to be an engineer, since you're good with math."

Because Walter's grandfather was blind, his parents sent Walter to see an eye specialist as a youngster to ensure his vision was not impaired. He later learned that he possessed an eye impediment that could be overcome with light, applied pressure, and additional focusing. Since this eye impediment was treatable, it would not hinder his ability to become a pilot. His parents focused on ensuring that he was properly prepared to become successful in life, whatever his career aspirations.

Davis eventually attended Ohio State University, studying electrical engineering. Since the school was a land-grant institution, two years of ROTC were required of each student. Davis was instantly attracted to the Navy ROTC candidates, and after finding out that several current members of the program had been recruited for membership, he asked the unit's CO why the recruiters did not recruit him. The CO, impressed by Davis' initiative, immediately offered him a position in the NROTC program.[62]

Significant Operational, Policy, and Technical Contributions

Fighter Section Leader, USS Constellation *(CVA 64)*

Lieutenant Commander Davis accumulated over 3,500 flight hours and made over 800 carrier landings as a fighter pilot. As fighter section leader in the mid-1960s, he led a section of aircraft on a night strike against the heavily defended Thanh Dam ferry crossing in North Vietnam. As his aircraft approached the target, several enemy antiaircraft batteries took it under fire. Disregarding the heavy barrage of antiaircraft fire, he skillfully searched the target area and discovered several enemy vehicles adjacent to the ferry. In spite of the distraction caused by flak bursting in close proximity to his aircraft, he made a precise dive-bombing delivery that resulted in two secondary explosions and the observed destruction of one of the vehicles. In another sequence, he completed twenty-five strikes and twenty-five direct combat-support missions against the enemy in an active combat area.[63] During this period, Davis made a significant impact on the success of the United States in carrying out its wartime mission. His innovative spirit in the face of enemy fire and under hazardous conditions speaks volumes about his courage and character.

Type Engineer for the F-14, Naval Air Systems Command

Commander Davis' exceptional dedication, superb technical skills, and creativity increased the weapons system capabilities and operational readiness of the F-14 aircraft. He aggressively led efforts to reduce F-14 material failures and incorporated changes and improvements through the acquisition system, resulting in a safer and more effective aircraft and weapon system. He led a joint Navy and contractor team that published a comprehensive "Conversion in Lieu of Procurement" study that provided planners with the information necessary to select accurately the most cost-effective aircraft alternative to meet the projected threats of the next two decades. Commander Davis' distinctive accomplishment had far-reaching and positive impacts on the operational capabilities of Navy F-14 fighters.[64]

Commanding Officer, USS Ranger *(CV 61)*

Captain Davis displayed inspirational leadership that was highlighted by the exceptional achievement and unprecedented levels of unit operational and material readiness. He often stressed personal initiative and professional excellence, and his contagious can-do spirit and genuine concern for the welfare of his men ensured the highest level of unit morale. His team achieved a fine reputation as a highly motivated, combat-ready team aboard a fully mission-capable aircraft carrier.[65]

Commandant, Naval District Washington, DC

Rear Admiral Davis' extraordinary vision and inspirational leadership were responsible for the achievement of a myriad of initiatives that greatly enhanced facilities and services provided to Navy activities and sea service personnel within the National Capital Region. His foresight and his integration and coordination of assets enabled the fulfillment of multiple assignment requests, including precise management of Navy space requirements and facilities and the improvement of quality-of-life services provided to military personnel.

Davis provided amazing support to foreign heads of naval service and other dignitaries and maintained unprecedented relations with local governments, civic organizations, and the foreign attaché corps. He was the preeminent ambassador of goodwill for the Navy in Washington, DC.[66]

Commander, Carrier Group 6

Rear Admiral Davis' superb leadership and innovation provided the catalyst for a record-setting Mediterranean cruise. He led the Navy's participation in Operation PROVIDE COMFORT TO SAVE the lives of Kurds in need. Admiral Davis set the standard for effective professional and personal relations with allies, which helped to advance Sixth Fleet concepts quickly. His innovative planning in numerous fleet-wide NATO areas enabled naval units under his operational command to meet all exercise and real-world objectives. This gained maximum benefit from training and furthered the positive image of the United States throughout the Mediterranean. He was the driving force behind the at-sea effort to counter narcotics trafficking into the United States.[67]

Director, Space, Information Warfare, and Command and Control

Vice Admiral Davis directed the modernization of the long-range, user-centered, C3 architecture known as "Copernicus" and was personally indispensable in developing its supporting strategy of Forward C4I for the 21st Century. He was the significant driving force behind the Challenge Athena initiative that leveraged commercial satellite communications to provide high-throughput connectivity to naval forces afloat and brought real-time information to the battlefield through an initiative known as the DoD Global Broadcast System. His innovative prowess revolutionized satellite communications, which moved C4I for the warrior into a new era of real-time information on the maritime and joint battlefields. He was directly responsible for implementing the Joint Maritime Command Information Strategy, and he pioneered the thrust to integrate modeling and simulation oversight into Navy mission-planning systems.[68]

Rear Admiral Macea E. Fussell

Background

Macea Fussell was born in Blackshear, Georgia, one of six siblings. He was reared on a farm that was passed down to his father after the original owner passed away. The farm provided a source of income and stability, and all six children were able to go to college.

When Macea was nine years old, he decided he wanted to become a doctor. He graduated as the valedictorian of his high school class and later graduated from Morehouse College in Atlanta. While he was in medical school, the Navy heavily—and successfully—recruited him for OCS. After his commissioning, he was stationed at Great Lakes NTC. Because there were so few African American officers in the Navy at the time, he was often mistaken for a CPO; even as a one-star flag officer later on, he was sometimes mistaken for a commander from a distance.

On the Great Lakes naval base, there was an extreme housing shortage, so Lieutenant Fussell had to pursue off-base housing options for his family. This presented a problem, as the housing surrounding the base was not available to African Americans. At the time, Fussell's wife was a few months pregnant, and when the CO found out about the housing issue off base he made arrangements for the Fussells to live on base. But Fussell refused the base housing, protesting, "If I can volunteer to serve this country, I should be afforded decent housing anywhere, not just on the base." He and some of his friends wrote a letter to the Secretary of Defense explaining the housing issue. The issue was not resolved, but Lieutenant Fussell believed he had to stand up for what was right, and Rear Admiral Fussell remains proud of the choice he made.[69]

Significant Operational, Policy, and Technical Contributions

Director, Health Services, Naval Reserve Readiness Command, Region Nineteen

Captain Fussell's superb leadership was key to REDCOM's attainment of exceptionally high medical readiness and the command's record of health professional support and retention. His expertise in Naval Reserve medical matters contributed significantly to unprecedented success in initiating and implementing programs in the training, readiness, and support of both reserve and active-duty forces.[70]

Force Medical Officer, Reserve Naval Construction Force (RNCF)

Captain Fussell demonstrated keen foresight and exceptional leadership in ensuring that the highest medical readiness was maintained for over 15,000 members of the RNCF. He was the driving force in ensuring that the personnel of two reserve naval mobile construction battalions recalled for Operations DESERT SHIELD and DESERT STORM were medically fit. Captain Fussell collaborated with the Bureau of Medicine and Surgery, the Veterans Administration, and other agencies to provide the best care to each individual, including by ensuring that he or she understood the specific illnesses affecting veterans of the Persian Gulf War.[71]

Deputy Pacific Fleet Surgeon, Pacific Fleet

Admiral Fussell's unsurpassed professional and medical competence ensured continuous improvement in all aspects of health care delivery throughout the Pacific Fleet. He led the participation of medical personnel in the KERNEL BLITZ 95 fleet exercise, the largest medical exercise since the end of the Vietnam War. He creatively designed and developed an urgently needed organizational structure that led to the establishment of the Commander, Naval Medical Forces Korea, which was pivotal in managing and overseeing the fleet hospitals being activated there. Admiral Fussell's changes in health policies reshaped the medical force of the future and instituted a major medical program realignment on the basis of total health care support readiness requirements.[72]

Rear Admiral Mack Gaston

Background

Mack Gaston was reared in Dalton, Georgia, by his grandparents. As the oldest of three boys, he was exposed to leadership early in life. His grandparents were not college educated, but they were the smartest people he knew.

After graduating from high school, Mack attended Tuskegee University. He worked his way through college, so he was a Tuskegee student during the day and a janitor at night. He eventually became head of the janitorial staff and instituted new ways to keep the facility cleaned.

Gaston was inspired to join the Navy because he did not think he would enjoy Army foxholes, and he considered the Navy more challenging than the Air Force. He was commissioned at the height of the civil rights movement, which presented unique challenges for him. However, his personality caused him always to view challenges as opportunities.

For example, when Gaston was a junior officer he was told to take an exam, and that for every question he got wrong he would have to stand an extra six-hour watch. After some time passed, he asked one of his colleagues, "How are the questions going?" The colleague replied, "What questions?" It was later revealed that Ensign Gaston had been singled out—no one else had to answer any such questions or stand extra watches. Yet even though the individuals responsible intended negative consequences for him, Ensign Gaston viewed the experience as an opportunity, because he was able to learn so much more than his counterparts about the ship and its crew. He is a strong advocate of maintaining a positive attitude regardless of circumstances.[73]

Significant Operational, Policy, and Technical Contributions

Director, Equal Opportunity Division and Special Assistant for Minority Affairs

Captain Gaston played a strategic and vital role in materially improving equal opportunity for all Navy personnel, thereby substantially enhancing the service's effectiveness and efficiency. He aggressively told the Navy story to national minority organizations, improving the Navy's image nationwide. His efforts greatly increased minority accessions, both in the officer and enlisted corps. He personally briefed flag officers on the newly implemented Command Managed Equal Opportunity Program, which increased the chain of command's understanding of and support in administering equal opportunity policies.[74]

Commander, Field Command, Defense Nuclear Agency

Admiral Gaston provided dynamic leadership in a time of diverse challenges for the nuclear community and DoD. His extensive background and forceful leadership provided the concept for the integration of test operations into the command, and he made total quality leadership the cornerstone of the command's changing and expanding role.

His innovative leadership led to flawless and successful testing of nuclear devices and their associated components via aboveground blasts, shock alignments, ground-motion assessments, and thermal radiation effects. His numerous contributions to the nation's nuclear arsenal have left a lasting influence.[75]

Commander, Naval Training Center Great Lakes, Illinois

While exercising brilliant leadership and superior professionalism in this position, Admiral Gaston made revolutionary improvements that have endured well into the twenty-first century. He was the architect of and driving force in establishing Great Lakes as the premier U.S. Navy training center. As area commander, Admiral Gaston led the full integration of Navy recruit training and established the foundation for the migration of enlisted warfare training, for men and women, to Great Lakes.

As the Midwest area coordinator, he annually provided superior management and oversight in budgeting and administration for over forty commands and activities that encompassed over 30,000 military and civilian personnel. As an ambassador to middle America, he ardently embraced the community and established partnerships that enhanced an understanding of the Navy's mission throughout a nine-state area. His far-reaching insight, unerring judgment, and unsurpassed loyalty dramatically improved the quality of training for the twenty-first-century sailor.[76]

Admiral Joseph Paul Reason

Background

Joseph Reason was born in Washington, DC, in 1941. His father and mother were both educators. His father Dr. Joseph Reason was a college professor and the director of libraries at Howard University and his mother Bernice was a high school science teacher. Because of childhood experiences fishing, swimming, and playing around water, Joseph developed a love for the sea. His parents were avid promoters of education; the young Reason spent most of his summers engaged in Boy Scouts of America programs and other educational experiences while attending summer camp on Lake Winnipesaukee in New Hampshire.

Reason became interested in NROTC in high school. He applied to the program but was not accepted, even though he ranked second out of 300 in his class of applicants. He attended three colleges prior to receiving a recommendation from Congressman Charles Diggs of Michigan that he apply to USNA. He understood that if he was accepted into the Academy his education would start anew—he would enter as a freshman. He graduated from USNA in 1965. He married Dianne Lillian Fowler three days later; their son graduated from the Academy in 1990.[77]

Midshipman Reason was interested in the prestigious nuclear power program, but to become a part of it a candidate had to pass a rigorous examination designed by "the father of the nuclear Navy," Admiral Hyman G. Rickover. Admiral Reason credits Admiral Rickover with assisting in his career; however, the initial meeting was a bit testy. Admiral Rickover was frustrated that Midshipman Reason's class ranking was not up to par, given that he possessed more prior education than many of his counterparts. The following contest ensued:

> Rickover told him that he could enter the training program if he promised to improve his class standing by twenty places. Reason kept his cool and responded that it was impossible to make a promise on that issue because no matter how well he performed, he had no control over the twenty students ahead of him. Rickover became furious at the cool and logical Reason and threw him out of his office. But Reason did not leave the building. Later, a different officer approached him with a note that read, "Admiral Rickover says you can have the nuclear power program if you will sign this statement that says, 'I swear I will increase my class standing twenty numbers by graduation.'" Reason looked at the statement, which guaranteed him entry into the much-coveted program—and crossed it out. In its place, he wrote: "I will do everything in my power to improve my class standing by twenty numbers." Rickover's aide tore up the paper and had his secretary type up the first oath again. Reason held his ground, knowing that otherwise he would be agreeing to accomplish something over which he had no control. For the second time in one day, he was thrown out of a high-ranking officer's office. But the next day, Reason's name was the third one posted on the list of candidates who had been accepted into the program.[78]

Significant Operational, Policy, and Technical Contributions

Electrical Officer, USS Enterprise *(CVAN 65)*

Under combat conditions, Lieutenant Commander Reason's tireless personal efforts and leadership maintained the highest state of material and operation readiness in the ship's electrical and aviation electrical support systems. His exceptional expertise and comprehensive understanding of all facets of his complex area of responsibility resulted in an unmatched record of systems reliability that provided *Enterprise* with a complete range of operational and support capabilities while at war. His creative leadership, foresight, and firm direction provided subordinates superb guidance under very demanding conditions and significantly contributed to the combat effectiveness of USS *Enterprise*.[79]

Naval Aide to the President

Commander Reason's astute leadership and perceptive judgment significantly contributed to his success in this highly visible position. He exercised continual and close contact with the highest officials of government, foreign and domestic, including the president, cabinet officers, agency heads, member of Congress, and foreign heads of state. He expertly coordinated several trips for the president around the world. His creativity was showcased as he superbly coordinated detailed arrangements for deployment and management of various DoD assets supporting complex logistical and scheduling requirements for the Oval Office.[80]

Commander, Naval Base Seattle, Washington

An extremely competent and resourceful leader, Admiral Reason was responsible for and directly led several missions while assigned as the regional coordinator and planning agent for all naval matters in Alaska, Washington, and Oregon. Through his dynamic leadership, he combined the effort of all regional shore commands toward the common goal of improving naval efficiency and productivity across the spectrum. His innovative leadership in working with the community to promote naval objectives was felt and welcomed throughout every major city in the region, with positive results for the Navy. His effort solidified the concept of regional coordination and developed a strong Navy and civilian team throughout the Pacific Northwest.[81]

Commander, Naval Surface Force, Atlantic Fleet and Deputy CNO (Plans, Policy, and Operations)

Admiral Reason efficiently and effectively improved every conceivable aspect of the warfighting abilities of Atlantic Fleet surface forces. His keen attention to the fiscal, material, personnel, and combat readiness of surface-force ships and units provided the nation with mission-ready assets that responded to taskings around the globe. Despite steady reductions in force levels and increases in commitments, Admiral Reason remained focused on the mission of putting ships to sea. His initiative, vision, and sage counsel as the Navy's operations deputy were of incalculable value to the Department of the Navy, the JCS, and the Secretary of Defense during a period of immense political turmoil.

As the president formulated responses to a series of crises in the Arabian Gulf, southern Europe, Africa, the Caribbean, and the western Pacific, Admiral Reason played a pivotal role in the derivation and execution of national security policy, which maximized the effectiveness of U.S. military intervention, while leaving nonmilitary options available to the National Security Council, the commander in chief, and U.S. allies.[82]

"I totally attribute my success to those who have gone before me—all minorities," said Adm. J. Paul Reason, the Navy's first African American four-star admiral. He commanded the Atlantic Fleet, headquartered in Norfolk, VA.

Rudi Williams

Commander in Chief, U.S. Atlantic Fleet

Under Admiral Reason's inspirational leadership, the Atlantic Fleet experienced unparalleled readiness and mission achievement throughout a period of intense operational commitments and institutional change. A visionary leader, he expanded operations with foreign navies, provided unsurpassed stewardship of limited funds, and restructured the Atlantic Fleet as a faster, quicker, and more effective organization. Admiral Reason's vision spearheaded the support for a CNO initiative to reduce unnecessary burdens placed on unit COs during the interdeployment training cycle. This resulted in the disestablishment of hundreds of inspections and organizations that had lost their value and the consolidation of needed programs and inspections into a single-look, once-a-cycle assist visit. Considered "the sailor's advocate," Admiral Reason, via his personal efforts, was key to significant improvements in the quality of working and living conditions throughout the fleet.[83]

Rear Admiral James A. Johnson

Background

James A. Johnson was born in North Carolina in the late 1940s. His parents migrated from the South to Chicago for increased opportunities. His mother was a social worker, his father a career postal worker.

Johnson's parents and extended family taught him three paramount principles, a foundation built from age three onward. The first was the expectation of college attendance. His father had earned his college degree, and his parents made clear from a very early age that college was mandatory. The next lesson was that he could choose any career, but whatever he chose he must be the very best at it. The last lesson was to go through life with honor and integrity; criminal behavior was not tolerated.

Johnson came from a proud tradition of trailblazers. His maternal aunt, a pioneering African American journalist, was honored with a U.S. Postal Service commemorative stamp. Another maternal aunt was the first African American principal in the Chicago public school system.

When he was six years old, James decided that he would become a doctor; he later concluded that his childhood bouts with asthma, which required trips to the doctor's office, fostered this decision. Years later, he earned his undergraduate degree in biology/chemistry from Oberlin College in Ohio and his medical degree from the University of Rochester in New York.

When James was fourteen years old, he was appointed the first African American page in the U.S. House of Representatives. However, after he reported, the appointment was rescinded; he later appeared on the *Today* show to speak about this experience.

Johnson always had a fascination with Navy ships, so when he finished college the Navy was a clear choice for him. He was commissioned in 1966 via the Ensign 1915 Program.

Johnson's first deployment in the Navy lasted eleven months. His first CPO sat him down and said, "I will teach you how to be a leader. You are senior to me and I salute you; however, I am also your teacher." This CPO remained Johnson's lifelong friend and confidant.

In the late 1960s, race riots were breaking out on several Navy ships, including Johnson's. In addition to being the senior medical officer aboard, he was also the only African American officer; the CO appointed him race relations assistant. Johnson was in charge of calming down the people on the ship. He gathered the men together and told them: "Men, I don't care who you are or what color you are, but if you try to do anything that will extend me at sea and keep me from seeing my family by way of sabotage, fighting, etc., then you are my mortal enemy. This would not be a good position for you, as I grew up on the south side of Chicago, plus I spent two years learning how to cut people." The race riots ceased.[84]

Significant Operational, Policy, and Technical Contributions

Assistant and Head, Surgery Department, Naval Hospital, Marine Corps Base, Camp Pendleton, California

Captain Johnson used his superior clinical competence and outstanding leadership expertise to modernize the hospital's main operation rooms with state-of-the-art surgical equipment that included all-new electrosurgical and electrocauterization equipment. Demonstrating compassionate, people-focused leadership, he was instrumental in procuring stapling equipment that reduced patient surgical time by approximately two hours per case.

As a commander, he assumed the role of Director of Surgical Services, a position that a senior Medical Corps captain normally filled. Practicing direct leadership in this role, he spearheaded a program to enlighten staff physicians on the intricacies of utilization-review and diagnostic-related groups. He also developed and initiated "economic grand rounds" to standardize physician care and improve physicians' understanding of the costs associated with treating and hospitalizing military beneficiaries.[85]

Deputy Chief, Navy Medical Corps and Surgical Specialty, Staff of the Surgeon General of the Navy

Captain Johnson's comprehensive analyses were instrumental in improving the structure of the Medical Corps. They provided the basis for key surgeon general decisions that significantly enhanced the readiness of the Medical Corps. By Johnson's direct leadership, the officer accession policy development program of the Bureau of Medicine and Surgery became a reality. This program dramatically improved effectiveness by ensuring optimal training utilization and diversity accountability.

Captain Johnson acted as a catalyst during Operations DESERT SHIELD and DESERT STORM by molding policy and ensuring Medical Corps readiness through properly trained, certified, and assigned surgeons and other physicians. He demonstrated visionary leadership in initiating and implementing a laparoscopic surgery project by coordinating procurement actions to obtain equipment and surgeon training, saving the government innumerable man-days and millions of dollars.[86]

Medical Director and Deputy Commander, Naval Medical Center San Diego

Captain Johnson's exceptional vision and dedication led to an enhanced, revitalized, and expanded level of quality health care for over 710,000 beneficiaries in the Region Nine Tricare catchment area. Exhibiting a cooperative spirit, he spearheaded an extremely successful civilian mentoring program that greatly supported and enhanced retention rates for numerous civilian employees. He also facilitated a resource-sharing agreement through the CHAMPUS [military health care program] Reform Initiative that saved over one million dollars and made an additional 140 full-time medical staff members available.

In addition, Johnson attracted and recruited into the Navy numerous high-caliber physicians, which resulted in the command receiving the distinguished Bureau of Medicine and Surgery recruiting award.[87]

Commanding Officer, Naval Hospital Bremerton, Washington

While in this capacity, Johnson innovatively guided the implementation of TRICARE in the Bremerton area and provided improved patient access and service quality, while simultaneously responding to fleet and UN operations requirements by deploying fifty members of his command to support HADR efforts in Haiti.

Johnson's deep concern for sailors and their families led to the construction of a primary-care clinic that resulted in the enrollment of 7000 additional patients, which saved the Navy approximately three million dollars in contract adjustments.

Johnson spearheaded efforts to employ information management technology throughout his organization by creating a local area network that included over 700 desktop computers with high-speed Internet access. This bold initiative developed a work environment that fostered data-driven decisions and saved innumerable man-hours.[88]

Rear Admiral Larry L. Poe

Background

Larry Poe was born and raised just outside Salisbury, North Carolina. His mother was a high school English teacher; his father was a blacksmith for the Southern Railway. Larry credits his mother with inspiring him most in life; she encouraged him to defy normal expectations for an African American child growing up in the 1950s. When he was fifteen, he asked his mother, "What should I be someday?" She replied, "I don't want to tell you what you should be, because that may become all you will be." In her unique way, she propelled him to reach for the stars, break barriers, and make history.

Poe attended a segregated high school but was offered several college scholarships. Because his roots were in North Carolina, he decided to further his education at Livingstone College in 1961. During this time, African American students who desired to attend a state-funded college had to petition the courts. After two years at Livingstone, he successfully petitioned the courts and transferred to the University of North Carolina—one of only five African American undergraduates enrolled as members of the class of 1965.

After graduation, Poe was commissioned an ensign and attended AOCS in Pensacola for a year. However, because he possessed the sickle cell trait, he was not allowed to complete flight school. He then elected to serve as an intelligence officer in the Navy. His first duty assignment was to Heavy Photographic Squadron 61, assigned to Seventh Fleet and forward-deployed to Da Nang Air Force Base in Vietnam.[89]

Significant Operational, Policy, and Technical Contributions

Vice Director of Intelligence, U.S. Atlantic Command

Rear Admiral Poe exemplified the full integration of reserve components into the joint team at USACOM. Besides providing sage advice and counsel to the director, his visionary leadership and advocacy of future joint intelligence requirements focused national attention and support on key issues such as the enabling concepts of federated battle damage assessment and collaborative precision engagement. His increased integration of reserve capabilities into USACOM's Joint Intelligence Center enabled it to expand production while downsizing its active-duty force.[90]

Commander, Office of Naval Intelligence

Taking over a critical command position on extremely short notice, Rear Admiral Poe's extraordinary leadership skills, professional competence, and in-depth understanding of the challenges facing our nation enabled him to guide ONI successfully during an important transitional period. During his tenure, ONI continued to provide the highest-quality, timeliest, and most reliable all-source maritime intelligence to fleet and national decision makers.

Poe's genuine compassion for people, belief in the importance of teamwork, and ability to prioritize intelligence requirements effectively resulted in a dramatic improvement in command morale, and also fostered enhanced relationships among ONI and other defense and national intelligence organizations.[91]

Principal Director and Acting Deputy Assistant Secretary of Defense for Intelligence

Rear Admiral Poe displayed truly visionary leadership and outstanding management skills while providing to OASD (C3I) the necessary planning, programmatic, and budgetary oversight to develop and implement a comprehensive restructuring plan for intelligence support to operations for the twenty-first century.

Additionally, Rear Admiral Poe established the Office for Reserve Support, thereby more effectively implementing programs to provide critical expertise and manpower to OASD (C3I) in support of national-level goals and objectives. An outstanding leader, he demonstrated the ability to understand the future environment and quickly develop plans and actions to achieve success.[92]

U.S. Defense Attaché, Paris, France

Rear Admiral Poe excelled in one of the most complex and challenging attaché positions in the world during an intense time in diplomatic and military relations between the United States and France. As the principal representative of the Secretary of Defense and CJCS in France, Admiral Poe was directly responsible for an increased level of cooperation, understanding, interaction, and interoperability with the French military. His polished diplomatic skills assisted in strengthening Franco-American military-diplomatic relationships through a difficult period of crises in Africa and the Middle East, as well as the conduct of the continuing GWOT. His exemplary service in a position of significant responsibility and the wide spectrum of his enduring contributions furthered the national security and foreign policy goals of the United States.[93]

Deputy DoD Inspector General for Intelligence

Serving as a catalyst for the transformation of the Office of Inspector General and defense intelligence restructuring and as counselor and confidant to the inspector general, Admiral Poe led organizational change that greatly improved the inspector general's ability to serve as the "eyes, ears, and conscience of the commander" and support defense operations worldwide. In addition, Admiral Poe was selected to serve as the inspector general to the personal envoy of the president of the United States to Iraq. As the primary U.S. coordinator for the National Anticorruption Strategy for postwar Iraq, his timely contribution brought institutional integrity to Iraq's national anticorruption strategy, affecting all areas of the reconstruction effort.[94]

Vice Admiral Edward Moore Jr.

Background

Edward Moore Jr., one of four siblings, was born to Edward Sr. and Freddie Hayes Moore of Little Rock, Arkansas. Edward was a teenager during the 1957 school desegregation crisis and personally knew the members of the soon-to-be-famous Little Rock Nine, black teenagers who successfully challenged segregation in the Arkansas educational system by integrating Little Rock Central High School. Nonetheless, during his adolescent years he was educated in all-black surroundings, attending segregated elementary and junior and senior high schools.

Moore's parents reared him in an environment in which respect and education were paramount. They also taught him that, despite the success of the Little Rock Nine, challenging the established cultural norms in the rural South might have dire consequences. Edward determined that, for the immediate future, achieving his dreams would be more likely to occur outside the South. Yet despite living in a segregated and underserved community, he never felt poor or inferior.

Moore's father had served as a steward in the Navy, rising to CPO during World War II. Later his father worked several jobs, but his principal employment was as a nursing assistant at the Little Rock Veterans Administration hospital. His mother was employed building communication and telephone cables.

During the 1960s, the Selective Service System provided the Army's main supply of manpower. Moore's father's sea stories influenced Edward to join the Navy instead of the

Army. Two months before graduating from high school, Edward enlisted in the Navy Reserve. His plan was to serve his two years, save money for college that the Navy would match, and return to Little Rock to pursue a career there. But during boot camp this plan changed when he took an exam to qualify for ROTC and passed with flying colors. Given this opportunity, and already having been admitted to several colleges, he decided to forge ahead, using a combination of scholarships, federal education loans, Navy pay, and a part-time college job to pay his education expenses. In return, he would serve in the Navy as an officer for three years—but with no intention of staying beyond that.

During high school and his first year of college, Edward applied for congressional nominations to USNA, but was turned down on both occasions. He understood that receiving a nomination during this time in American history would be very challenging, but this did not deter him. With a full appreciation that a college education might offer more opportunities for success in life, he persisted and graduated from Southern Illinois University, Carbondale, Illinois, in June 1968.

After commissioning, he served on USS *Severn* (AO 61) as a junior officer. There he encountered an enlisted sailor from Mississippi who refused to obey Moore's order because was an African American. The sailor told him that his father had allowed him to join the Navy with the caveat of "not ever following the orders of an [N-word]." Ensign Moore asked the sailor whether he would accompany him and explain his refusal to the XO, and the sailor replied, "Sure!" After the sailor repeated for the XO why he would not carry out Ensign Moore's order, the XO gathered together the ship's yeoman and chief MAA, then called the CO. The CO held captain's mast on the spot, and three days later the sailor was discharged from the Navy. This provided a strong message to the crew that, despite the "oddity" of having an African American in the wardroom, challenges to good order and discipline would not be tolerated. His command's support encouraged Ensign Moore, as it suggested to him that the Navy valued teamwork, performance, and results without regard to ethnic background.[95]

Significant Operational, Policy, and Technical Contributions

Commanding Officer, USS Lewis B. Puller (FFG 23)

While commanding *Puller* (assigned administratively and operationally to Commander, DESRON 23), Commander Moore demonstrated innovation and creativity in guiding his command through several predeployment workups, a rigorous and highly successful deployment to the western Pacific, and numerous interdeployment assessments and inspections. His leadership in the command was recognized widely through his superior accomplishments while assigned to the USS *Enterprise* (CVN 65) task group. He was widely respected throughout DESRON 23 for his technical expertise, tactical knowledge and innovation, and meticulous planning.[96]

Assistant Chief for Manpower and Personnel Commander, U.S. Pacific Fleet

Captain Moore's performance was distinguished by initiative, innovation, and foresight in the areas of manpower utilization, fleet personnel readiness, civilian personnel, commercial activities, and human resources management. He was responsible for all manpower and personnel issues for 1,500 shore stations, 231 ships, 97 aviation squadrons, and over 203,000 military and civilian personnel. His innovative actions ranged from the expert establishment of an efficiency review program for shore facilities at the major-claimant level to the realization of actual savings in operations and staff of 410 million dollars and 1,100 billets through commercial activities. Through his direct efforts over a period of four years, twelve carrier battle groups deployed at a maximum state of personnel readiness.[97]

Commanding Officer, USS Cowpens (CG 63)

Captain Moore creatively assembled and trained the precommissioning crew of this *Ticonderoga*-class guided-missile cruiser and prepared its members to prevail through the full spectrum of inspections required to certify *Cowpens* as fully prepared for introduction into the Pacific Fleet. Employing dynamic leadership and superior managerial skills, he inspired his team to superior levels of performance during *Cowpens'* maiden deployment to the Arabian Gulf, including serving for three months as the anti-air warfare commander during Operation SOUTHERN WATCH. During this deployment, Captain Moore led a successful four-ship Tomahawk missile strike against a sensitive Iraqi target.[98]

Commander, Cruiser Destroyer Group 3 and Commander, Carl Vinson Task Group

Admiral Moore's extraordinary leadership resulted in the flawless execution of over 1,800 combat missions in support of Operation SOUTHERN WATCH, thirty-one Tomahawk land-attack missile launches in support of Operation DESERT STRIKE, the simultaneous orchestration of Joint Exercise RUGGED NAUTILUS, and one hundred merchant ship board-and-search operations in support of UN sanctions against Iraq. His task force made significant and lasting contributions to the future of fleet operations through the development of innovative force-employment plans, including the simultaneous use of Navy Tomahawk land-attack missiles and Air Force B-52-launched conventional cruise missiles, as well as the development of strike plans for future contingency operations.[99]

Assistant to the Deputy CNO (Plans, Policy, and Operations)

Admiral Moore represented the Navy with great skill in numerous joint, combined, and interagency forums. His innovative ability to pilot operational and administrative matters expertly through the appropriate headquarters and fleet channels significantly contributed to the protection of U.S. national interests around the globe. His accomplishments included executing successful noncombatant evacuation operations in Albania and Sierra Leone; enforcing UN sanctions against Iraq and the former Yugoslavia; concluding productive navy-to-navy staff talks with key allies and strategic partners; and preparing Navy positions on the Anti-Ballistic Missile Treaty, the START II Treaty, and the Chemical Weapons Convention in preparation for the Helsinki summit between President Clinton and Russian President Yeltsin.[100]

Commander, Naval Surface Forces, Pacific Fleet

Vice Admiral Moore's dedication to sailors and their families made this aspect one of his top priorities while serving in this capacity. While coordinating the training and readiness of eighty-three surface ships and over 40,000 personnel, he spearheaded innovative initiatives, such as the CNO's interdeployment training cycle workload reduction effort, as well as successful crew rotations of ships assigned to forward-deployed naval forces. This total commitment to quality-of-life initiatives and service to sailors resulted in significant improvement in enlisted retention and savings of over twenty million dollars for the Navy. He was significantly involved with changing the manner in which Navy ships prepared for forward-deployed operations. Under Admiral Moore's guidance, his staff eliminated extraneous bureaucratic requirements that detracted from mission accomplishment and ensured that COs possessed flexibility in preparing their crews for naval warfare and mission accomplishment.[101]

Vice Admiral David L. Brewer III

Background

David Brewer was born in 1946 in Farmville, Virginia, but was raised in Orlando, Florida. His mother and father were both educators who met while attending Booker T. Washington's Tuskegee Institute. His grandparents were graduates of Tuskegee in 1912. Thus, education was a foundational legacy and principle in the Brewer household.

David eventually attended Prairie View A&M University, which in 1968 established the first NROTC program at an HBCU. Initially, this unit was considered an "experiment" to see whether an HBCU could produce quality naval officers. The program started with twenty-one midshipmen, thirteen of whom continued after the initial summer screening and vetting. Thirteen midshipmen were commissioned, ten Navy and three Marine Corps. Of the ten Navy officers, eight remained on active duty for twenty or more years. Of the eight, five achieved the rank of captain (O-6), and the sixth, Brewer, retired as a vice admiral. With six of the eight having been promoted to captain or higher, this promotion rate remains among the highest in the history of NROTC. Thus, the "experiment" was obviously a success, along with that at other NROTC units at HBCUs that produced quality naval officers. Since its inception, Prairie View A&M University has produced three African American admirals, more than any other college or university in the nation, with the exception of USNA.

When Brewer was commissioned in May 1970, there were 256 African American officers among the 72,000 officers in the Navy. Needless to say, most people in the Navy had never seen an African American naval officer, and in some cases reacted accordingly. Brewer's first assignment was as the electronic warfare officer aboard USS *Little Rock* (CLG 4), homeported in Newport, Rhode Island. One evening he went to the officers' club but was told he could not drink there. When he produced his identification, he was served. He filed a complaint with his chain of command. It was determined that the staff was not necessarily racist, but did not know black officers existed in the Navy. He never had a problem with that officers' club again.

However, during his early career Brewer did encounter blatant racism. One of his COs during his recruiting tour would refer to him as "that [N-word]," and his early fitness reports (performance evaluations) reflected those sentiments. However, for every leader who was biased, Brewer encountered several more who were fair and helpful to him. He recalled the following experience:

> I had been a recruiting officer for over three years and did not have much operational experience when I returned to sea duty for my second shipboard tour on board the USS *California* (CGN 36). My first at-sea watch was absolutely terrible because I lacked operational experience. The captain, realizing my potential, made the highly unusual decision to place the XO on watch with me until I was proficient. This captain could have let me fail, but he took a personal interest in helping me to succeed. This captain (who retired as an admiral) and I are still close friends today.

In 1981, Brewer was assigned as the chief engineer on the USS *Okinawa* (LPH 3). This assignment would prove to be his most challenging. He was the third chief engineer assigned to the ship within a year—the others had been fired. *Okinawa's* engineering department was considered to be one of the worst in the fleet. The captain, however, was very supportive. Brewer realized very quickly that the engineering department personnel needed positive leadership and a boost in morale. So he met with the CO and asked for his assistance in helping his men receive flag (admiral) letters of commendation as opposed to CO's letters of commendation, since the former counted as points toward promotion. He also asked the CO to give "spot" Navy Achievement medals for exceptional performance.

However, early in this tour, racism raised its ugly head again: Brewer learned that some of his white CPOs had said they would not work for "that [N-word]." Brewer later said, "I could have put an already low-morale department through an investigation and probably fired them, but chose to show them leadership despite their racism." As a result, the engineering department performed well, its reputation was resurrected, and some people whose careers had been at a dead end got promoted because of his award system. Those "racist" CPOs became some of his biggest supporters. During this challenging tour, Brewer "earned his chops" and learned he could be a good naval officer.

However, certain biases persisted in the Navy, even years later. In 1994, shortly after reporting for his first flag officer tour, in Guam, he was jogging in his neighborhood (Flag Circle) when an MAA pulled his car in front of him, got out of the vehicle, and told him he could not run there. After telling the sailor that he was "the Admiral" and lived in the flag quarters, the MAA immediately apologized. Vice Admiral Brewer, very frustrated over this incident, directed his chief of staff to call the base commander and have his picture posted everywhere on the base to prevent any recurrence of this embarrassing incident in the future.

Thanks to great leadership, the Navy evolved with respect to its treatment of African American officers, who increased in number from 256 in 1970 to over 3000 in the 2000s. Admiral Brewer says many of his mentors were white officers who were forthright in their support of him and other African American officers, resulting in a dramatic increase in African American senior and flag officers.

Admiral Brewer's leadership philosophy of being a "ladder builder" as opposed to a "ladder climber" informed his success throughout his naval career. Ladder climbers are self-centered and concerned only with individual achievement; ladder builders are focused like a laser on the success of their subordinates. This leadership style is based on the foundational principle that you are only as successful as the success you create in others. According to Admiral Brewer, "Worry about creating success in your sailors, then your success will take care of itself."[102]

Significant Operational, Policy, and Technical Contributions

Junior Officer, USS California (CGN 36)

Lieutenant Brewer demonstrated exceptional professional knowledge and attention to detail. He significantly contributed to the overall success of the task force's efforts by developing a special operational data-formatted message, which was adopted and used during multiple training exercises. During Joint Exercise SOLID SHIELD 1977, he also developed a challenging matrix of operational codes and a new method of surveillance area reporting for his command. He consistently arrived at and promulgated correct tactical decisions relating to air-defense actions.[103]

Commanding Officer, USS Bristol County (LST 1198)

Commander Brewer led his command to receipt of the Battle Efficiency "E" as the best LST in the Pacific Fleet. A superb ship handler, he directed the ship's successful salvage of a downed Coast Guard helicopter off the coast of Baja, California, and a successful rescue of four Marines whose CH-46 helicopter crashed at night on the flight deck of an amphibious assault ship.

Brewer was the innovative inspiration for the successful Adopt-A-School Program and for Bristol County's unprecedented "Super Goal Buster" performance in the 1986 and 1987 Combined Federal Campaigns.[104]

Special Assistant to the Chief of Naval Operations

Captain Brewer's thorough knowledge of the Navy's Equal Opportunity Programs and close coordination with national minority-affairs organizations made him a valued personal adviser to the CNO. Under his leadership, the Navy's diversity efforts were expanded and opportunities for reaching underserved populations in America were prioritized.[105]

Commander, U.S. Naval Forces Marianas/Representative of CINC, U.S. Pacific Command to Guam/Northern Marianas/Federated States of Micronesia/Republic of Palau

Admiral Brewer displayed exceptional skill and innovative insight in this important assignment by dealing superbly with a wide range of complex and politically sensitive issues that have a direct impact on the U.S. defense relationship throughout Micronesia. His creative approach to education in the development of several innovative programs improved the quality of education for all the children of Guam.

Brewer's diplomatic skills were showcased during a highly publicized port visit to Vladivostok, Russia, where his staff contributed to the festivities celebrating the fiftieth anniversary of the end of World War II in the Pacific. He effectively led a team to respond to the Republic of Palau's declaration of emergency when a collapsed bridged severed all water and power sources to an area of the country. He also capably, and eloquently, coordinated the receipt, processing, and further movement of over 2,700 Kurds fleeing from Iraq to seek asylum in the United States. As a result of his innovative leadership and creativity, USPACOM civic action teams achieved unprecedented successes and contributed to the accomplishment of USPACOM's cooperative engagement mission.[106]

Commander, Amphibious Group 3

Admiral Brewer's exceptional accomplishments and innovative leadership were directly responsible for dramatic improvements in the combat readiness of his forces. His aggressive and visionary approach resulted in both technical and training enhancements that facilitated the deployment of every amphibious ready group with fully manned, trained, and integrated crews. His group was poised and ready to meet expeditionary warfare demands from Kuwait to Korea.[107]

Vice Chief, Naval Education and Training

Admiral Brewer's sound judgment, innovation, and proactive leadership style positively influenced every aspect of Navy education and training. He led the development and execution of the Navy college program, the Information Technology University, and the Navy Learning network. These educational concepts vastly improved individual academic achievement and overall organizational readiness. He worked with several colleges in communities across the country to provide bachelor's and associate's degree information to almost 300,000 sailors.

As the innovator in the executive review of the Navy training working group, he was the driving force behind the revolution in Navy training. His conceptualization of the 21st Century Sailor played a vital role in the coordination and implementation of major improvements to training facilities and technology that realized significant cost savings and reduced the impact of personnel shortages. He orchestrated creative training initiatives that made 4,388 sailor work-years available to the fleet through reduced course length, lower attrition, and more efficient student processing.[108]

Commander, Military Sealift Command

Under Admiral Brewer's exceptional leadership, MSC flourished. He facilitated its effective deployment of combat logistics support for multiple forward-deployed carrier strike groups and expeditionary strike groups for the GWOT. Following the September 11th terrorist attacks, he immediately activated USNS *Comfort* (T-AH 20) to provide onsite support to disaster relief workers at Ground Zero during Operation NOBLE EAGLE. He masterfully led the largest continuous movement of combat cargo since World War II for Operation IRAQI FREEDOM. His ships formed the "steel bridge of democracy," delivering more than eighty-three million square feet of combat vehicles and supplies and nearly eight billion gallons of fuel to U.S. warfighters in Iraq and Afghanistan.

Vice Admiral Brewer also directed lifesaving responses to the Indonesian tsunami and to hurricanes that ravaged the U.S. Gulf Coast.

A transformational leader, Brewer aligned five worldwide area commands and their type commander functions into a single type command that is now the Military Sealift Fleet Support Command.[109]

Rear Admiral Osie V. Combs

Background

Reared in a small Texas town, Osie Combs attended Prairie View A&M University. After commissioning via NROTC, he experienced setbacks owing to discrimination, but believed he had to stay the course for the sake of others to follow. Admiral Combs was a trailblazer who paved the way for up-and-coming leaders in today's Navy.

As a lieutenant commander, Combs relieved as repair officer on a tender, a position a captain had filled previously—an extraordinary accomplishment.

Combs was the project manager in charge of building two thirds of the early 688-class submarines. He built the USS *Houston*, the first submarine commanded by an African American.[110] Admiral Combs' brilliance in designing submarines left a lasting legacy on the Navy and the country.

Significant Operational, Policy, and Technical Contributions

Program Manager, Large-Scale Vehicle (LSV) Program, Naval Sea Systems Command

Commander Combs' outstanding technical knowledge, visionary leadership, and superb administrative ability yielded tremendous benefits for the Navy. He was responsible for and directly supervised the design and construction of the LSV and its support facilities. The LSV was used to verify and refine the design of the *Seawolf*-class submarine to meet the challenge of the next generation of quiet Soviet submarines. Commander

Combs dedicated countless hours of temporary additional duty to supervising the ongoing work personally, leading a team of industrial and naval engineers in the construction of the world's largest unmanned, computer-controlled, free-swimming submersible; the construction of a modern support facility; the development and construction of a dedicated radiated noise facility; and the development and installation of a test range. Facing unique challenges, such as constructing the LSV without the benefit of experienced shipbuilders, moving the massive LSV from its construction site to the test site via rail, and directing its test phase, Commander Combs skillfully, smoothly, and flawlessly directed the program to delivery. His efforts significantly contributed to new knowledge in the submarine design process.[111]

Assistant Program Manager for Design and Construction, Seawolf *Acquisition Project*

Commander Combs made significant improvements in the design and construction techniques for the *Seawolf*-class submarines. He overcame austere fiscal environments in orchestrating available funding and the talent pools of responsible organizations to manage *Seawolf*'s design and construction to meet the program's stringent specifications. He displayed impressive perseverance and insight in developing and implementing plans that managed several diverse activities responsible for completing *Seawolf*'s design and construction. While directing members of the Naval Sea Systems Command submarine technical community, he significantly improved their understanding and focus on the design, development, and construction issues associated with the first nuclear U.S. attack submarine design in twenty years. His creativity and meticulous attention to detail provided his team a clear vision of the proper precepts to guide submarine development and construction.[112]

Vice Commander, Chief Engineer, and Program Director for Command, Control, Communications, Computer, and Intelligence Systems, Space and Naval Warfare Systems Command

Rear Admiral Combs was the primary motivational factor in bringing to fruition the command's mission to deliver supported, affordable, integrated, and interoperable world-class information solutions to warriors to enable them to dominate today and in the foreseeable future. Under his aggressive, results-oriented leadership, SPAWAR established the chief engineer position to define overall architectures and system-engineering solutions to provide a direct interface with the waterfront.

Combs accepted the challenge from CINC U.S. Pacific Fleet to revamp fleet IT for the twenty-first century. He developed an integrated implementation plan that was in use within fifteen months, when the first Information Technology for the Twenty-first Century (IT-21) battle group deployed.

Despite contending with an 18 percent reduction in command size and a personnel turnover of 80 percent, he significantly contributed to establishing SPAWAR's organizational structure and procedures as the command physically relocated from the east to the west coast as a result of a 1995 Base Closure and Realignment Commission decision.[113]

Rear Admiral Gene Kendall

Background

Gene Kendall was born in rural—and segregated—North Carolina. His parents were children of sharecroppers and neither graduated from high school; his father quit school in the sixth grade to assist his parents on their farm.

Yet although his father was not formally educated, he taught his son the value of upward mobility, often saying, "If you don't like where you are, then don't be in the same spot tomorrow." His mom taught him the value of perseverance and that the sky was the limit for reaching his dreams.

As a youngster, Gene loved the library—he would often "get lost" inside—and this led to a love of reading. Reading about Booker T. Washington and George Washington Carver inspired him to think beyond his socioeconomic situation and dream of accomplishing similar feats. But as a product of segregated schools, Gene studied from textbooks handed down from the local white schools.

Kendall performed well in high school, but realized that his parents could not afford to send him to college. So, backed up by a lot of prayer and hard work, he applied for and received a scholarship to Duke University. He was one of the first five African Americans admitted to Duke, in 1963. (A million-dollar scholarship endowment remains at Duke to commemorate their attendance.) The scientific and engineering workload at Duke was very challenging; he did not complete the program.

But after leaving Duke, Kendall was determined to redeem himself, and this became a driving factor behind his entry into the Navy nuclear community. When Kendall first entered the Navy as an enlisted man, his aspirations were to achieve the rank of E-5. However, this changed once he saw a photo of Commander Samuel L. Gravely when Gravely was in command of USS *Taussig* (DD 746); this moment changed the trajectory of his life. After serving in the Navy for a couple of years, Kendall attended the University of Kansas under the Nuclear Engineering Commissioning Program, majored in physics, and graduated with honors.

Kendall credits his mentors with ensuring he met the correct milestones in his career. Early on, when race riots were occurring on several naval vessels, he became the race relations officer as a junior lieutenant. He was flown to several different commands to enforce the new race relations policy. Higher authority directed him to go undercover to infiltrate the gangs on his ship; however, his CO would not permit it, which Kendall credits with saving his life. Admiral Kendall later became a mentor himself, and one of his mentees was Midshipman Michelle Howard, who would later become Vice CNO.

During his tour at the Surface Warfare Officer School in Newport, Rhode Island, Kendall was the founding director of the engineering officer of the watch course and director of the engineering specialty training course. He went on to become the special assistant to the CNO in Washington, DC, where he helped guide the Navy's policies in the area of equal opportunity and minority affairs.

Kendall assisted the Navy in determining its best course and strategy over the next twenty to thirty years as a fellow with the CNO Strategic Studies Group (SSG) XV at the Naval War College in Newport. This group called for deep, conceptual thinking about warfare, accompanied by action plans for tracking purposes. Concepts such as the rail gun, net-centric warfare, offshore mobility platforms, and cooperative engagement strategies were conceptualized during his time on SSG XV.[114]

Significant Operational, Policy, and Technical Contributions

Commanding Officer, USS Fletcher (DD 992)

Commander Kendall demonstrated exceptional leadership, providing the driving force behind the completion of numerous inspections and distinguished visits whose success exceeded expectations.

Kendall's team surpassed every underway commitment, including two PACEX deployments. A renowned ASW tactician, his operational prowess and ability to locate submarines directly influenced his crew and earned them the distinction of best detection and classification team in the ASW squadron; his team surpassed all other ships in PACEX 89.

His personal attention to and promotion of high personal standards and professional growth throughout the ship resulted in numerous officer qualifications and the highest number of enlisted surface warfare qualification designations in recent history.[115]

Deputy Director of Operations, National Military Command Center

Rear Admiral Kendall directly contributed to the coordination and execution of essential strategic national security policy. He played a vital role in executing military events across the globe, including operations in Bosnia-Herzegovina, humanitarian relief efforts for Cuban migrants, de-escalation of tensions on the Korean Peninsula and in the Taiwan Strait, and noncombatant evacuation operations in Albania, Sierra Leone, Zaire, and Republic of the Congo.[116]

Director, Fleet Commander in Chief Liaison Division, Staff of Deputy CNO

Rear Admiral Kendall provided outstanding leadership and commendable innovation, demonstrating a comprehensive and intuitive understanding of the Navy's planning, programming, and budgeting systems and the fleet's entire spectrum of priorities, requirements, and issues. As the CINC's primary representative on the CNO's staff, he ensured that support and liaison to the fleet was timely and comprehensive, meeting every operational need. He directed and facilitated the fleet CINC's integration into and participation in the integrated warfare architecture process, as well as subsequent development of the CNO's program assessment and program objective memorandum.[117]

Vice Admiral Adam M. Robinson Jr.

Background

Adam Robinson was born in Louisville, Kentucky. Robinson's family understood the power of education even before 1900: his grandfather finished college in 1890, receiving a degree in Greek and Latin studies. Around the end of the Spanish-American war, his grandfather took the civil service exam; he became a postal worker in 1901, and maintained that position for thirty-five years. His grandmother was employed as a schoolteacher and social worker; she ensured Robinson's father attended medical school at Howard University, from which he graduated in 1937. Adam's parents met in college. Robinson's father was a family medicine doctor and surgeon in Louisville, Kentucky, from 1945 until he died in 1969.

Adam Robinson would eventually follow his family's path of embracing education. He was accepted into the Indiana University School of Medicine in Indianapolis through the Armed Forces Health Professions Scholarship Program. Following the completion of his surgical internship at Southern Illinois University School of Medicine, Springfield, he was commissioned in the U.S. Navy. Eventually he became the thirty-sixth surgeon general of the Navy.[118]

Significant Operational, Policy, and Technical Contributions

Ship's Surgeon, USS Midway *(CV 41)*

While serving as ship's surgeon, Lieutenant Commander Robinson contributed significantly to the development of mass-casualty procedures and the training of medical emergency-response teams. His leadership significantly improved the combat readiness and capability of *Midway* and Carrier Air Wing 5. His efforts led to the outstanding performance of battle dressing stations and emergency medical teams during *Midway's* 1983 operational readiness evaluation that observers graded the "best ever." Lieutenant Commander Robinson led an exceptionally responsive emergency medical-assistance team that was directly responsible for saving crewmembers' lives, and his commitment to medical excellence was unsurpassed, serving as an inspiration to all who observed him.[119]

Staff Colorectal Surgeon, Naval Medical Center Bethesda

As the command's sole colorectal surgeon, Commander Robinson expertly ran a busy colorectal service with a volume of over 200 endoscopies monthly. He innovatively conceived and installed a state-of-the-art video endoscopy suite. In total, he directed the provision of complex and sophisticated surgical patient care to over 1,200 patients monthly. He implemented creative management techniques to improve accessibility to care by 20 percent, which reduced appointment delays and improved the quality of care.

Commander Robinson's ingenuity led to a significant contribution to the surgery residency program, which directly contributed to the careers of over thirty young Navy general surgeons and countless other providers.

Robinson's participation in the community and in dialogue within numerous committees and national surgeons' organizations significantly enhanced the image of Navy medicine.[120]

Commanding Officer, Naval Hospital Yokosuka, Japan

Captain Robinson used commendable innovation and demonstrated superior leadership in directing the outstanding delivery of quality health care services to tens of thousands of forward-deployed sailors and their families assigned to U.S. installations from the western Pacific to the Indian Ocean. Following the incidents of September 11th, he ensured the U.S. naval hospital and ten diverse Navy medical clinics were fully prepared and capable of supporting U.S. military and coalition forces assigned to this forward-deployed base during Operation ENDURING FREEDOM.[121]

Commanding Officer, Fleet Hospital Jacksonville, Florida

Captain Robinson, a proven and dynamic naval health care executive, provided outstanding health service support for American forces, UN and American embassy personnel, and the citizens of Haiti. Captain Robinson ensured the seamless provision of medical support during the five-month absence of the American embassy physician. He led more than seventy humanitarian assistance missions and provided needed medical care to more than 20,000 Haitian citizens. He also facilitated a critical incident debriefing of 135 Argentine personnel following a tragic helicopter crash.[122]

Director, Medical Readiness Division, Bureau of Medicine and Surgery

Captain Robinson championed the reassignment of operational control of fleet reserve hospitals to the Navy's surgeon general. This significantly contributed to the military's concept of total force integration by seamlessly deploying reserve units in support of active-duty troops. He created an expeditionary medicine division that focused organizing resources to ensure Navy medicine met the needs of naval warfare operations in the twenty-first century.

Under Robinson's leadership, various "tiger teams" addressed innovative ways to improve the worldwide operation of blood banks, strengthen the peacetime operations of naval hospitals and clinics, and address the stress that military life places on warfighters, support personnel, and family members.[123]

Surgeon General of the Navy Vice Adm. Adam Robinson speaks with Joint Detention Group personnel during a tour of Joint Task Force Guantanamo, 29 March 2008. Robinson visited the JTF to meet with health care providers and tour the detention facilities.

JTF Guantanamo photo by Navy Petty Officer 2nd Class Patrick Thompson

Surgeon General of the Navy

Vice Admiral Robinson's visionary leadership as thirty-sixth surgeon general of the Navy ushered in new comprehensive-care models that focused on patients and provided family-centered care. This carefully orchestrated system expertly balanced the dual mission of providing readiness for thousands of sailors and soldiers deployed to war zones while maintaining world-class care at home. His innovative leadership can be measured in lives saved—the lowest battlefield mortality rate in history—and in globally strengthened medicine partnerships. His dedication to and genuine concern for sailors, Marines, and their families served as a model for all future surgeons general.[124]

Rear Admiral Lillian E. Fishburne

Background

Lillian Fishburne was born in Patuxent River, Maryland; she has one sibling. Both of her parents were high school graduates, and her father was offered a college scholarship—but his mother convinced him to refuse it because accepting it might be perceived as charity. Lillian's father was a Navy hospital corpsman, and as a Navy dependent she moved all over the world. This traveling exposed her to the Navy and the military's way of life, but during high school and college she had no aspirations to join the Navy; she wanted to become a social worker.

During her last year of college her brother became ill, so she stayed home during the subsequent summer to assist in his recovery. Her parents eventually convinced her that they would care for her brother, and encouraged her to attend to her own career goals. She left for New York City to pursue a career in social work.

Lillian took a job while preparing for the social worker entrance exam. While awaiting the results of the test, she was given an unfair evaluation in her current job. This caused her to explore other opportunities; for example, she previously had taken the federal test for post office employment, and she followed up to learn the results. But after inquiring about the post office, she spoke to a Navy recruiter about other opportunities. The Navy recruiters were very impressed with her, so they shuttled her off to take an exam, and she was accepted into the Navy the same day. She attended and was commissioned via OCS.

In 1973, while working as a junior officer, a male first class petty officer walked into her office and told her, "I will never salute a woman officer." She replied, "You don't have to salute me, but you will salute this uniform." She encountered similar situations throughout her career, and she always provided immediate feedback to correct the behavior.

Rear Admiral Fishburne credits her mentors with providing the guidance necessary to choose the jobs and make the hard decisions that led to upward mobility throughout her career.[125]

Significant Operational, Policy, and Technical Contributions

Navy Recruiting District, Miami, Florida

Even as a lieutenant (junior grade), Lillian Fishburne demonstrated superior achievement in the performance of her duties: while at this command, she was presented the Gold Wreath Award on numerous occasions. It is presented to individuals who demonstrate exceptional fortitude and determination; it forecasts a continued ability to excel. Lieutenant (junior grade) Fishburne demonstrated the epitome of achievement, and her professionalism, dynamic leadership, and total dedication to any assigned task were certainly a part of her formula for success.[126]

Navy Service Representative to the Command Systems Integration Agency

Commander Fishburne was directly responsible for advising the director on sensitive matters pertaining to the Navy's unique processing systems and procedures. She participated as the Navy representative before the term "jointness" had been coined. Her innovative approach to command, control, communication, and information-processing systems and procedures catapulted technically superior solutions to the forefront in the naval service.[127] This extensive understanding of unified and complex issues during the pioneering era of the joint operating concept showcased her intellect and abilities.

Commanding Officer, Naval Computer and Telecommunications Area Master Station

Captain Fishburne's commendable innovations and inspiring leadership resulted in unprecedented levels of responsive fleet communications and computer applications support across the Navy. In addition, she championed a number of technological and facility upgrades, many of which were performed by command personnel, in conjunction with state and local community coalitions. Her meticulous attention to detail as the regional commander resulted in flawless communications support throughout the Pacific theater.[128]

Director, Information Transfer Division, and Deputy Director and Fleet Liaison, Space, Information Warfare, Command, and Control for the CNO

Rear Admiral Fishburne brilliantly spearheaded the development of the Navy's C4 program budget proposals, resulting in significant resource investments in support of the Information Technology for the 21st Century program. Her strong leadership and managerial acumen were essential to programmatic success while advancing 21st Century initiatives throughout the budget process to launch the highly innovative Navy and Marine Corps Intranet. Demonstrating exceptional breadth of knowledge of war-fighter requirements, she was a powerful advocate for inclusion of innovative technologies and methodologies in support of the Navy's role in Joint Vision 2010 and 2020. Her exceptional and enduring contributions to the formation of C4 planning and requirements definitions ensured the Navy would be optimally positioned to incorporate ongoing and anticipated advances in IT.[129]

Rear Admiral Willie C. Marsh

Background

Willie Marsh was born in a small town in Alabama. He was one of two siblings and was reared on a farm. His family did not have much money, but the farm provided the necessities of life. His grandfather was a farmer whose work ethic had a huge impact on Marsh's life. His grandfather taught him to be the best at any endeavor, and that "your word is your bond."

Willie was exposed to being a second-class citizen throughout his adolescent years, as Jim Crow laws prevailed everywhere in his community. To survive during this time, African Americans had to tolerate segregation.

Willie's grandfather only finished the seventh grade; Willie's parents were high school graduates; Willie was the first in his family to attend college. An avid lover of books throughout his life, he used reading as a mechanism to escape the socioeconomic facts of life in his community. But he also developed an inquisitive nature and acquired an unquenchable thirst for knowledge.

Marsh did not consider the Navy as an option until he was well into college. During his freshman year at Alabama A&M University, he was exposed to Vietnam-era protests. At several universities, protesters succeeded in removing the ROTC presence from campuses. This did not occur at Alabama A&M; in fact, the university started a new Army ROTC program during his sophomore year. Marsh attended the informational session, but after learning about the program he was not interested in joining the Army.

However, the instructor informed him that he could go into another service after completing the Army ROTC program, if that was his desire, so he joined up. During his senior year, his Army ROTC instructors again tried to convince him to join the Army, but were not successful.

At that point, Marsh submitted a Navy package and was accepted. Marsh credits Admiral Gravely and his mentorship for his choice of the Navy for a career. The two had met at a gathering at the admiral's home and a wonderful relationship developed. Marsh observed that the Navy was serious about promoting African American officers; he saw the greatest opportunity for advancement in that service.

Marsh's junior-officer years were similar to the experiences of other future African American flag officers: he experienced workplace isolation, had few mentors, and did not find many individuals to whom he could relate. He encountered individuals who did not want to take orders from him because of his race, but he also received support from his command to challenge and correct this behavior. His desire to be the best in any endeavor fueled him to look past injustices and accomplish great things for the Navy.

These included operations when he was CO of USS *Sumter*. He deployed five days after taking command, with orders to proceed directly to Liberia to respond to the guerilla uprisings of the late 1980s. His task was to evacuate U.S. nationals who were in harm's way; he and his team evacuated over 900 personnel to safety in Sierra Leone.[130]

Significant Operational, Policy, and Technical Contributions

Branch Head, Chief of Naval Education and Training

Commander Marsh personally enhanced the engineering readiness of the fleet by coordinating the management oversight effort between the CNO and the Naval Education and Training Command (NAVEDTRACOM, or CNET). He led the development and implementation of the CNET firefighter trainer certification program, which ensured that 170,000 Navy personnel at eleven training centers received safe and realistic training. He was the driving force behind the standardization of firefighting and damage control training under CNET's aegis. He aggressively coordinated and implemented the entire damage control and firefighting lessons learned from the USS *Stark* (FFG 31) and USS *Roberts* (FFG 58) incidents into NAVEDTRACOM training programs.[131]

Commanding Officer, USS Cleveland (LPD 7)

Captain Marsh's "Seven Star" philosophy (training, teamwork, safety, mission, cleanliness, professionalism, and battle readiness) secured his command's unqualified success and superior operational efficiency. He demonstrated charisma and commendable innovation while leading his ship through a highly successful western Pacific/Arabian Gulf deployment, which included Operations SOUTHERN WATCH and VIGILANT SENTINEL. His drive and vision brought *Cleveland* the distinction of two consecutive battle efficiency awards and its sixth consecutive Allen G. Ogden Award.[132]

Commander, Task Force 51

Admiral Marsh's visionary leadership was instrumental in the coalition's rapid victory in the liberation of Iraq. He expertly orchestrated and executed lethal naval force projection and off-loaded combat power to support more than 50,000 U.S. Marines. As commander of the largest amphibious task force since World War II, his amphibious ships supported more than 2,600 combat sorties and effectively delivered ordnance onto a wide range of targets, which proved pivotal in expediting the rapid advance on Baghdad. His initiative and attention to detail were responsible for the successful defense of the seaport of debarkation and gas and oil platforms critical to the humanitarian relief and economic viability of a postwar Iraq. Through his innovative and transformational combat leadership, his task force met or exceeded all mission taskings supporting the victory in Iraq.[133] This included providing the leadership that orchestrated the rescue of Private First Class Jessica Lynch.

Rear Admiral Vinson E. Smith

Background

Vinson E. Smith, a native of Carthage, Tennessee, graduated in 1969 from Gordonsville High School, and in 1974 from Tennessee Technological University. After his commissioning via AOCS, he reported to the precommissioning unit for USS *Nimitz* (CVN 68). After completing his surface warfare qualifications, three division officer tours, and three deployments in *Nimitz*, he completed two years at the Naval Amphibious School, Little Creek, Virginia, as an instructor.

Smith completed department head tours as operations officer in USS *Charles F. Adams* (DDG 2) and weapons officer in USS *Luce* (DDG 38). As a department head, he deployed to the North Atlantic with the Standing Naval Force Atlantic and to the Arabian Gulf during the Iran-Iraq tanker war of the 1980s. Following his joint duty assignment, Smith assumed command of USS *Robert G. Bradley* (FFG 49) in October 1992. During his tenure, the ship was awarded the safety award and three consecutive battle efficiency awards. In August 1994, he returned to the COMNAVSURFLANT staff as the combat systems/C4I officer. Smith assumed command of Naval Station San Diego in February 1996.[134]

Significant Operational, Policy, and Technical Contributions

Assistant Chief of Staff for C4, Naval Surface Force, Atlantic Fleet

Captain Smith demonstrated his resourcefulness and impressive devotion to duty in coordinating over thirty separate mechanical, electrical, and combat systems ship visits into a combined combat systems readiness review that saved the taxpayers millions of dollars while ensuring peak equipment operability and maximum efficiency for every deploying ship in the Navy. He creatively restored the CNO's Command Maintenance Program funding, which supported all combat systems in the Navy and consolidated maintenance procedures throughout the fleet.[135]

Commanding Officer, Naval Station San Diego, California

Captain Smith demonstrated commendable innovation in managing the daily operation of the largest shore installation in the Pacific Fleet. He creatively applied analytical techniques and scrutiny that maintained a firm grasp on the execution of an operating budget of over forty-nine million dollars and attained an unsurpassed obligation rate of 99 percent. He significantly improved operational capabilities and the quality of life for thousands of sailors, investing over 143 million dollars in facility maintenance projects. He also oversaw the successful completion of over 450 self-help projects, which saved twelve million dollars.

Captain Smith personally was the driving force behind the monthly oil spill working group. He initiated an effective oil spill program and an aggressive environmental program that diverted over 26,000 tons of solid waste from local landfills and yielded revenue of over two million dollars.

Smith was the architect behind the merger of Naval Station San Diego and Transient Personnel Unit legal departments, which saved taxpayers over 80,000 dollars annually.[136]

Commander, Naval Surface Group, Pacific Northwest

Rear Admiral Smith's masterful strategic planning and wise use of Navy assets demonstrated his outstanding leadership and resourcefulness. He was responsible for the third-largest fleet concentration area, which encompassed all naval activities within Washington, Oregon, Idaho, and Alaska. He created the first material processing center, which enabled all ten surface group ships to deploy on time and in fully mission-capable condition. He collaborated with the private sector to provide quality housing through a public-private venture that became a Navy prototype for innovation funding. His innovative leadership was evidenced when his region was the first in the Navy to receive a five-star accreditation for all bachelor housing by CINC, Pacific Fleet and the award of the 2002 Installation Excellence Award.[137]

Rear Admiral Reubin B. Bookert

Background

Reubin Bookert was born in Columbia, South Carolina, in 1950. He was reared in a two-parent, two-child home. His father maintained two jobs; his mother was employed as a nurse. Although his parents were not college educated, they were hardworking individuals. Money was scarce, but Reubin never felt poor. He attended segregated schools, and these institutions taught him lifelong lessons about character, dignity, and self-respect. The combination of his teachers' influence and his parents' teachings formed the foundation of his character.

When he was fifteen years old, Bookert decided that he would join the Navy, influenced by a presentation that Midshipman Charles Bolden gave at C. H. Johnson High School; Bolden eventually become a general officer in the Marine Corps. Bolden's father was Bookert's guidance counselor. Upon graduation from high school, Bookert went to North Carolina A&T University. After graduating he worked in industry for AT&T. After a couple of years, he decided to contact a recruiter and join the Navy via OCS.

The first few years as a junior officer were rough for Bookert. He was one of only two African Americans aboard the ship and mentors were few, so he had to figure out how to become successful independently. Often, conversations in the wardroom would change abruptly or stop when he entered, and sometimes when the ship visited a foreign port the other officers would go on liberty without him. This treatment empowered Bookert to study harder and be the best at any task assigned. While most of his colleagues used the department heads as mentors to assist with their qualifications, he qualified with minimal support.

After leaving his first command, things got markedly better in terms of mentoring by his superiors. This caused his outlook on the Navy to change considerably, and he began to make significant positive progress professionally. Because of his personal experiences, Bookert understands the value of mentoring, of reaching back to enable others to achieve their dreams. He is very grateful to the U.S. Navy for the opportunities it provided him.[138]

Significant Operational, Policy, and Technical Accomplishments

Commanding Officer, USS La Moure County (LST 1194)

Commander Bookert's ship provided unprecedented support and dedication during a coup d'état in a region of Gambia. His ship provided refuge to the U.S. ambassador and the president, vice president, and cabinet members of Gambia during an uprising by the Gambian national army and its eventual ouster of the installed democratic government and takeover of power. His quick thinking, level-headed decisions, and wise counsel to the ambassador prevented potential bloodshed, helped stabilize a volatile political situation, and ensured the safe return of four of his crewmembers who had been stranded ashore during the initial phase of the coup. His team kept the U.S. national command authority fully informed of the Gambian conflict as events unfolded, providing the only link to Washington and serving as its sole source of information.[139]

Special Assistant to the Chief of Navy Personnel

Demonstrating innovative leadership and initiative, Captain Bookert initiated dramatic and lasting improvements to equal opportunity programs for sailors throughout the Navy and vigorously pursued important initiatives to eliminate sexual harassment. He completely revised the Navy's equal opportunity manual and improved the Navy's equal opportunity and sexual harassment training. He creatively implemented key recommendations from an equal opportunity task force review and developed long-range strategies for improving minority accessions and retention. Captain Bookert provided comprehensive briefings to members of Congress and played a vital role in promoting a positive Navy image in the civilian community.[140]

Deputy Director, Expeditionary Warfare Division

Admiral Bookert's extraordinary leadership resulted in the superb management of naval expeditionary warfare. He managed approximately forty billion dollars across the Future Years Defense Plan in various programmatic appropriations. He championed resources for expeditionary warfare and maintained twelve LPD-17 programs needed to regain the lift capability for 2.5 Marine expeditionary brigades. He also provided an urgently needed antiterrorism/force-protection capability to the fleet. As an advocate of transformational underwater unmanned vehicle technology, Admiral Bookert greatly enhanced mine warfare and protection capabilities.[141]

Rear Admiral Barry C. Black

Background

Barry Black grew up in the inner city of Baltimore, Maryland, when segregation was alive and well in the United States. (His neighborhood was portrayed accurately in the HBO series *The Wire.*) He did not meet or shake hands with a white person until he was sixteen years old.

Black was raised by his mother, the daughter of a sharecropper, who possessed a fourth-grade education. After relocating to Baltimore, she worked as a domestic to care for her seven children. She joined the Red Temple, a Christian church in the neighborhood, which became the beacon of hope for Barry and his six siblings. Thus, Rear Admiral Black does not come from a family of pedigree; but he credits being born in a democracy—where his merits rather than his heritage or other affiliations were rewarded—for his successful career.

Black possessed a passion for young people, so he attended seminary. After graduation, he pastored a church in Durham, North Carolina. One day two sailors traveled all the way from Jacksonville, North Carolina, to Durham to hear him preach. After speaking to them about why they had traveled over a hundred miles to hear him speak, they informed him that they had never seen an African American chaplain. This intrigued him, and he decided to join the Navy because of the opportunities to reach youths and make a difference.

After joining the Navy, Black experienced the challenge of overcoming stereotypes applied to ethnic minorities; on one occasion, a superior called him [the N-word]. He understood that some individuals brought their personal baggage with them to the workplace and he had to learn how to deal with that. Yet his experience was similar to that of other African American flag officers, in that for every person who meant him harm, there were three or four who helped him. Admiral Black possesses a biblical worldview whereby he sees God as being the ultimate judge who is in complete control of his destiny. In his worldview, each person is a part of the larger human race rather than a particular race defined by ethnicity. This worldview has had a lasting effect on him, and he credits it with allowing him to overcome obstacles and attain upward mobility in his professional career.[142]

Significant Operational, Policy, and Technical Contributions

Fleet Chaplain, CINC, U.S. Atlantic Fleet

Captain Black provided superb leadership to the 153 chaplains and 133 religious program specialists in the Atlantic Fleet. His innovative leadership led to a major reorganization of fleet and force chaplain resources, creating two new ministry directorates that produced comprehensive strategic planning and new initiatives for waterfront ministry.

Black coordinated a bold new joint ministry training program, procuring 40,000 dollars to assist in creating electronic avenues available to chaplains in all the military services. He pioneered a mentoring program for junior officers with 100 percent participation by Atlantic Fleet chaplains.

Captain Black delivered more than twenty-six superb lectures and addresses on ethnic awareness and equal opportunity throughout the continental United States and overseas.[143]

Chairman, Armed Forces Chaplains Board, Office of the Assistant Secretary of Defense for Force Management Policy

Rear Admiral Black provided visionary leadership to promote and ensure the free exercise of religion and improve the quality of life for the entire armed forces community. Under his leadership, a comprehensive review of the policies and procedures DoD used to screen prospective ecclesiastical endorsing agencies was completed.

Admiral Black spearheaded a program of interservice training and drilling participation for reserve component chaplains and enlisted religious support personnel. Owing to Admiral Black's distinctive accomplishments and ingenuity, coordination efforts with the Civil Air Patrol, Veterans Administration, and international chaplaincies greatly expanded opportunities for joint and multinational religious ministry and triservice chaplain interoperability.[144]

Chief of Navy Chaplains

Rear Admiral Black served as a strong, visionary force for the Chaplain Corps and the Navy. His covenant leadership and uncompromising emphasis on operational readiness enabled active-duty and reserve chaplains to respond to a broad range of religious and pastoral needs of sailors, Marines, and their families in the aftermath of the terrorist attacks of September 11th and in support of extended combat deployments during Operations ENDURING FREEDOM and IRAQI FREEDOM.

Rear Admiral Black's focused, long-term efforts, articulated in a forward-looking strategic plan, organized the chaplain corps to support and achieve the CNO's top five priorities. The enduring effect of his inspirational presence was evidenced further by the transformation of the Chaplains' Religious Enrichment Development Operation into a mobile resource to serve forward-deployed sailors and Marines.[145]

Vice Admiral Derwood Curtis

Background

Derwood Curtis was born in Japan and was adopted by his American family when his father, a member of the Army, was stationed overseas. When his father returned to the United States, Derwood's family settled in the Washington, DC, area. Owing to family issues, Derwood attended five different elementary schools, but still developed a deter-mined work ethic and good habits.

Involvement in the Safety Patrol, sports, and Cub Scouts was instrumental to teach-ing Curtis discipline and to keeping him out of trouble. Derwood was always a top performer in Cub Scouts, and his den mother, who served the scouts for twenty-nine years, was very inspirational. She taught him valuable lessons about honor and integrity, and always to "Do your best!" She was also den mother to J. P. Reason, who became the Navy's first black four-star admiral, and she was very serious about mentorship. Cub Scouts gave Derwood a sense of accomplishment; he was given a uniform, leader-ship positions, and an honor code to follow. As a member of Cub Scouts, he became acquainted with Army personnel, and also became the captain of the Safety Patrol. Altogether, this area of his life had a huge impact on him.

Derwood was inspired to consider future military options because of his father's Army portrait that sat on a table by the front door. Curtis was also fascinated when watch-ing television programs that depicted Army soldiers engaged in combat, seeing movies depicting ancient Roman and Greek warfare, and studying books on the general subject.

After moving from Washington, DC, to Chicago, Illinois, Curtis attended high school, where he immediately enrolled in the Army JROTC program and joined the football team, student council, and honor society. At that point, he was interested in becoming a West Point cadet. He became captain of the football and track teams and eventually battalion commander of the JROTC unit, leading over 350 students. His football coach was another inspiration; he encouraged him to attend USNA because of its unique program and the future opportunities it offered—the coach thought it would be a great fit for Derwood. A football recruiting trip to USNA immediately convinced Curtis it was the place for him.

Only seventy-seven African Americans entered USNA with him in 1976, of whom thirty-four would receive their commissions four years later. This was the largest group of African Americans to graduate from the Academy since 1845; it put the cumulative number of such graduates over one hundred. At USNA he was a member of the color guard, and the upperclassman above him would eventually become CNO; Vice Admiral Curtis would become commander of naval surface forces under that officer's command. At the Academy, he excelled as an athlete and became a regimental commander.

On his first ship, Curtis faced many challenges of racism, prejudice, and lack of acceptance. Even after serving a successful subsequent Academy tour, winning the Arleigh Burke Award as the top student at Surface Warfare Officer School, and maintaining an extremely positive attitude, there were many roadblocks. But with hard work, discipline, a true belief in God, and good personnel, Curtis took on the hard jobs, met the challenges, overcame adversity, and soared to the Navy's highest ranks. Along the way, he made an impact on and inspired many. He was promoted early and given early command, and he eventually held seven command positions—something few have ever achieved. He was the eleventh African American admiral to achieve three stars in the history of the U.S. Navy.

Over the course of his career, Curtis spearheaded war efforts for Operation Desert Shield/Desert Storm, reinvented ASW warfare with his work in net-centric ASW, revitalized fleet training and maintenance, strategically improved safety and security in West Africa, improved military relationships with Russia, promoted the Navy's newest warship, and mentored many officers and enlisted personnel along the way.

Vice Admiral Curtis credits his wife for her undying support, his high school football coach for believing in him, his history teacher for challenging him, his pastor for spiritual guidance, and his den mother for teaching him to "Do your best!"[146]

Significant Operational, Policy, and Technical Contributions

Commanding Officer, USS Donald B. Beary (FFG 1085)

Commander Curtis assumed command of this vessel on extremely short notice owing to the untimely relief of his predecessor. He immediately infused a renewed and positive sense of mission, enthusiasm, and professionalism throughout the crew. His creativity and inspirational vision were responsible for the demonstrated superior performance of his command. Through his constant efforts to realize and maintain the highest level of operational, maintenance, and training readiness, he ensured that Beary was poised to be an instrument of national power.[147]

Curtis masterfully planned, coordinated, and effected a tremendously successful inspection and survey visit that set the standard for units within Surface Group 6. After taking command, his ship outperformed all other assets in a wide range of training exercises.[148]

Staff, Under Secretary of Defense for Acquisition and Technology

While serving as a member of the staff, Captain Curtis provided amazing oversight of naval warfare programs during a period of extensive departmental downsizing and recapitalizations. He used his impressive technical expertise, extensive operational command experience, and creative talent to coordinate multiple department activities in preparing for the milestone decision for the Surface Combatant of the 21st Century and Cooperative Engagement Capability programs. He vastly improved and expanded communications between the Office of the Secretary of Defense staff and its Navy counterparts.[149]

Commander, Destroyer Squadron 14

Captain Curtis' superior leadership and war-fighting expertise contributed significantly to the national interest by fully supporting fleet commanders around the world. As the maritime force commander during the Black Sea exercise SEA BREEZE 1998, which involved twenty-seven warships from fourteen nations, his innovative leadership served to strengthen Partnership for Peace relationships within the region.

Curtis' exceptional supervision of the development of the Navy's net-centric ASW concept assisted both Second and Third Fleets with new technology that impacted future capabilities, doctrines, and tactics.

A proven, dynamic, and aggressive at-sea commander, he commanded a decisive opposition force that always provided challenging war-at-sea concepts for three battle groups during their predeployment workup cycles.[150]

Naval Aide to the Secretary of the Navy

Captain Curtis' superior performance, personal loyalty, and unmatched professionalism were of extraordinary benefit to the Secretary of the Navy. He consistently ensured the secretary was thoroughly prepared for top-level meetings and a wide variety of policy, planning, programming, and acquisition matters.

Present in the Pentagon during the terrorist attack of September 11th, Captain Curtis demonstrated uncommon presence of mind in supervising the evacuation of the secretariat and the reconstitution of a crisis action center around the Navy Annex.[151]

Commander, Naval Surface Group 2

Admiral Curtis demonstrated superb expertise, vision, and innovation in leading the Navy's largest surface combatant group of ships and two destroyer squadrons. Under his leadership, the command attained unprecedented levels of combat readiness and performed superbly in every national security commitment.

Curtis was the waterfront leader in the Mayport, Florida, and Pascagoula, Mississippi, Navy components, both of which experienced improved retention, quality of service, and community relations. His exceptional grasp of geopolitical and military issues was invaluable to U.S. engagement in the Western Hemisphere.[152]

Commander, Carrier Strike Group 11

Admiral Curtis led his strike group to the highest level of readiness and tactical proficiency, always pushing the innovation envelope in C2, tactical Tomahawk employment, and use of unmanned air and surface vehicles. He exhibited inspiring leadership and extraordinary operational skill across a wide tactical spectrum during the composite training unit exercise. This resulted in marks of "superior" from Commander, Strike Force Training Pacific.

As the combined forces component commander for RIMPAC 2004, his staff of 150 officers and enlisted personnel successfully deconflicted a challenging airspace control plan and coordinated over 3000 air training sorties involving aircraft of a seven-nation coalition in support of the joint force commander. This exercise was labeled the most successful exercise in the three-decade history of RIMPAC. Additionally, he established the *Nimitz* strike group human performance syndicate, which provided a terrific forum for exchanging ideas and best practices.[153]

Director of Navy Europe Programs, Resources, and Support and Director for Transformation Activities for Commander, U.S. Naval Forces Europe Sixth Fleet, Rear Adm. D. C. Curtis, gives an athlete a soccer ball after completion of a community relations project involving submarine tender USS *Emory S. Land* (AS 39). *Land* was conducting training exercises and community relations projects with host nationals while on deployment to the Gulf of Guinea.

U.S. Navy photo by Photographer's Mate 3rd Class Aimee N. Tortorich (Released)

Director, Navy Europe Programs, Resources, and Support

Admiral Curtis transformed this command, providing superb oversight of the transition from geographically and functionally separate echelon 2 and echelon 3 staffs into a single coherent operational staff in Naples, Italy. His innovation and determination expedited the completion of major-threat transformational projects, which not only generated current-year savings of fifty million dollars but also enabled U.S. Naval Forces, Europe to capitalize on current capacity and increase theater security cooperation initiatives.

As the leader of Navy Europe's engagement strategy, he was vital to strengthening relations with our enduring partners, including Germany, Russia, and Greece. Among other accomplishments, his efforts helped ensure Russian Navy participation in Operation ACTIVE ENDEAVOR for the first time. Displaying extraordinary strategic vision and unparalleled dedication, he was the driving force behind the Navy-hosted, U.S. European Command-sponsored Gulf of Guinea Maritime Safety and Security Workshop in Accra, Ghana. This unprecedented conference provided an important forum for maritime leaders from West Africa, Europe, and the United States to discuss opportunities for cooperation and enhanced maritime security in the Gulf of Guinea region.[154]

Commander, Naval Surface Forces

Vice Admiral Curtis' brilliant innovation, inspiring leadership, flawless senior executive skill, and unequivocal loyalty to Harris transported the first wave of Marines to Iraq in sthe sailors and families of the U.S. surface Navy resulted in unmatched success. With visionary leadership, he provided warships ready for tasking to the combatant commanders, effectively manning, training, equipping, and sustaining a combined force of 163 ships, fifty-three special combat support force units, and sixty-four subordinate staffs around the world. His surface force met every mission and achieved superior operational results through his meticulous execution of a 7.3-billion-dollar operational and maintenance budget and unequaled leadership of over 60,000 military and civilian personnel. He implemented bold and strategic changes through his back-to-basics philosophy that charted a course to improve the long-term health and sustainment of the Navy's surface ships and their sailors.[155]

Rear Admiral Julius S. Caesar

Background

Julius Caesar was born and raised in Blacksburg, Virginia; he had one sibling. Although his parents were not college educated, his mother understood the value of education and ensured he performed well academically during his adolescent years.

Julius' father, a friend of Alma Gravely, owned and operated a tailoring business called Caesar's Dry Cleaners that had been opened in 1901 in Radford, Virginia, and passed down by Julius' grandfather. His maternal grandfather also owned a business: he sold candy and ice cream treats—which were made available to all children, not just an elite few. His grandfather had witnessed African American children saddened by receiving ice cream that was already melted because the law restricted African Americans from entering the front door of an eating establishment, and this motivated him to start his operation. Both of Julius' grandfathers, as respected business leaders in their small-town community, played a key role in influencing his life.

Caesar was an outstanding athlete in high school and was recruited by USNA Coach Steve Belichick (father of New England Patriots football coach Bill Belichick). Julius' father encouraged him to apply for the Academy because of the GI Bill and other fringe benefits available via the military. When he entered USNA in 1973, Julius was part of the largest influx of African Americans ever; but he is the only African American admiral from that class.

As a junior officer Caesar was, like most of the other future flags, the only African American in the wardroom, but he and his Academy colleagues worked together and accomplished great things on his first ship.

In 1983, Caesar transferred to the Naval Reserve and played a pivotal role in supporting air-defense operations.[156]

Significant Operational, Policy, and Technical Contributions

Commanding Officer, Naval Reserve, Surface Warfare Division, Staff of Deputy CNO

Captain Caesar played a significant role in institutionalizing the area air-defense commander system into the Naval Reserve to support fleet theater air-defense operations. The establishment of these units and initiation of the training and professional requirements within a six-month period was unprecedented.

He displayed outstanding initiative, delivering over 10,000 man-hours to support numerous surface warfare initiatives and fleet exercises, which enhanced mission accomplishment of both programmatic and surface warfare community goals.[157]

Commanding Officer, Naval Reserve, Naval Inspector General Detachment 106

Captain Caesar demonstrated exceptional creativity and leadership. He was the driving force behind the elimination of a backlog in excess of 400 hotline cases, an achievement never attained previously in the Hotline Division's twenty-year history. He delivered 300 days in support of command inspections and area visits by empowering a team of highly trained inspectors and encouraging high-tempo operations. He was instrumental in establishing a new reserve staff competency in evaluating the Navy's cost-management practices, which supported the Secretary of the Navy's "Revolution in Business Affairs." He also developed a comprehensive case-management information system handbook to enhance productivity of the Hotline Division, its staff, and its Reserve support.[158]

Deputy Commander, Navy Reserve Readiness Command

Captain Caesar demonstrated unparalleled resourcefulness as he spearheaded a highly successful national training program for 900 COs. Under his inspiring leadership, REDCOM's medical readiness increased from 79 to 85 percent and in-assignment processing time decreased by 20 percent. He led a strategic planning effort to accomplish the historic merger of sixteen operational support centers and 7000 personnel with Commander, Navy Region Mid-Atlantic. He skillfully organized a regional mentoring program and a Campaign Drug Free Program that reached more than 23,000 local youths. Captain Caesar was a significant contributor in addressing force structure, readiness, and total force strategy issues.[159]

Vice Director, Joint Concept Development and Experimentation, U.S. Joint Forces Command

As acting director, Admiral Caesar demonstrated inspiring leadership and skill when the Secretary of Defense announced his recommendation to disestablish the command.

Admiral Caesar was the driving force in planning the reorganization of the directorate. He quickly and efficiently organized the mission analysis and contingency planning needed to assess the courses of action associated with maintaining, transferring, or eliminating core experimentation functions. He adeptly led 550 military, government, and contractor personnel to perform the U.S. Joint Forces Command mission while managing a hundred-million-dollar budget during a period of great austerity and transition.

Admiral Caesar served as flag champion for the Ballistic Missile Defense Phased Adaptive Approach Project and led the Joint Concept Development and Experimentation Enterprise executive committee to approve sixty-eight initiatives for incorporation into the CJCS FY 2011 experimentation campaign plan. He demonstrated consummate international diplomacy in transitioning products for the Multinational Experiment 6 Campaign, involving eighteen nations and NATO allied command transformations. As a result of his efforts, U.S. Joint Forces Command successfully validated results and used them to transition into meaningful change that informed joint doctrine, leadership, education and training, and policy guidance.[160]

Vice Admiral Anthony L. Winns

Background

Anthony Winns was born in 1956. His family moved from Arlington, Georgia, to the Jacksonville, Florida, area when he was about two years old. His mother, an educator, was the most important figure in his life. She instilled in him the drive and motivation to be successful.

Anthony's first real interaction with Caucasians came in 1969, during a national Boy Scout jamboree in Idaho. Only two black Boy Scouts from the city of Jacksonville were chosen to participate. His experience to that point had been formed by the Jim Crow laws of the South, under which "colored only" and "whites only" signs were commonplace.

Anthony grew up attending segregated schools until the tenth grade. Upon desegregation, African American children were bussed to schools to which they were assigned alphabetically; he went to Ed White High School in Jacksonville. Upon reporting to this suburban, majority-white school, the new textbooks he received surprised and delighted him; prior to this, he had seldom seen a new textbook in school—those he was accustomed to using were often second- and third-generation books, with pages torn out.

Anthony's tenth-grade school schedule was selected for and mailed to him. He noticed that he was not enrolled in a math class. The school was "unable to assist him" in redressing this. So he skipped Algebra I in tenth grade, then enrolled in Algebra II and Geometry during his junior year to compensate for the missed class.

During his senior year, he attended a USNA midshipman's presentation that encouraged him to apply for a congressional nomination to the Academy. He was accepted, and in 1978 became a distinguished graduate.

As a young, newly commissioned ensign in the naval aviation community, workplace isolation was not uncommon for the young officer. He would sometimes get a five-minute warning prior to participating in certain social events, even though the event had been underway for hours. However, his southern experience base proved beneficial in dealing with certain attitudes in the Navy. While serving as a lieutenant on an aircraft carrier in 1983, he spoke of the following experience:

> We were on a dependents' day cruise, and there were several older gentlemen on board. I was on the bridge, driving the ship as officer of the deck. I recall a conversation between my skipper and an elderly retired flag officer. I vividly remember the older gentlemen saying to my skipper that our country should gather up all the blacks and send them back to Africa. I was stunned to hear this conversation on the bridge. After the retired gentleman had departed the bridge, my skipper inquired whether I had heard the gentleman's comments. I replied, "Yes sir." My skipper apologized for the flag officer's comments, and said it was not appropriate and they were certainly not aligned with the Navy's or his personal beliefs. I replied, "Sir, you don't have to apologize to me. I grew up in the South, and I've heard and lived through worse. If I had allowed comments like that deter me from my goals, I would not be here today."

Winns went on to become the highest-rated officer among his peers on the ship, and his CO handwrote and underlined in his fitness report, "He will be a flag officer."

Winns never forgot the incident on the ship's bridge. Similar to the approach taken by most of his flag colleagues who came up during this time in American history, he chose to make it a motivating factor to succeed in the Navy, not a hindrance to success. Winns became the first officer in his USNA class to be selected for rear admiral, in May 2000.[161]

Significant Operational, Policy, and Technical Contributions

Assignment Officer, Naval Personnel Command

As a young lieutenant, Winns demonstrated creativity that led directly to significant improvements in aviation officer distribution. Lieutenant Winns' creativity and extensive knowledge of the officer distribution system significantly enhanced aviation officer career development. His innovative spirit developed solutions to deal effectively with mid-grade officer shortages, training pipeline management problems, and unprogrammed fiscal constraints.[162]

Special Projects Officer, Patrol Squadron 11

Commander Winns provided superb leadership to over 380 men and women on two extended deployments to the Mediterranean and Caribbean. His innovation and creative spirit enabled him to coordinate the implementation of a revolutionary ASW system. Skillfully meshing the efforts of myriad naval and civilian personnel worldwide, he facilitated the exhaustive development of the fleet-wide system training curriculum.[163]

Primary Action Officer, CNO Working Group

Commander Winns coordinated the congressionally mandated Commission on Roles and Missions of the Armed Forces. He significantly contributed to the development of the Navy's position and rationale. This process was vital, and demanded extraordinary political judgment and professional knowledge to derive consensus across a broad range of issues important to the Navy. He used exceptional analytical and superb writing skills to ensure that arguments reflecting the unique capabilities and enduring functions of naval forces were well crafted and coordinated.[164]

Commanding Officer, USS Essex *(LHD 2)*

Captain Winns' innovative and dynamic leadership propelled his ship to accumulate awards that included the All Warfare Areas Award, Battle "E", Supply Blue "E", Admiral Flately Award First Runner Up, and the Type Command Top Financial Performer Award. In 1997, his ship became the only Pacific Fleet ship to certify in engineering training during Phase 1 of the Tailored Ship Training Availability.[165]

Commander, Patrol and Reconnaissance Force, U.S. Pacific Fleet

While serving in his initial flag tour, Admiral Winns developed, planned, and executed the transformational alignment of the maritime patrol reconnaissance aviation (MPRA) group into a more-efficient, combat-ready, and operationally relevant force. His innovative leadership resolved severe MPRA aircrew shortages that had continued for more than a decade. He also executed 23,475 mishap-free flight hours during 2,451 sorties in support of Operation ENDURING FREEDOM for Afghanistan, Iraq, and the Philippines. He became the first MPRA officer to act as combined forces air component commander for a RIMPAC exercise that ensured the safe execution of a twenty-eight-day flying program for fifty-eight dissimilar naval and air force aircraft from five nations.[166]

Staff, Deputy Chief of Naval Operations

Admiral Winns' creativity advanced the naval aviation requirements within the framework of Sea Power 21 and played a significant role in developing the future fleet of manned and unmanned aircraft to ensure maritime dominance for the United States. Admiral Winns orchestrated the critical bridging of legacy capabilities into several transformational platforms supporting crucial Sea Shield concepts and capabilities, ensuring naval aviation's continued relevance and war-fighting contributions well into the twenty-first century.[167]

Vice Director and Acting Director for Operations, the Joint Staff

Admiral Winns' creativity and stewardship resulted in the granting of approval for sensitive and complex special forces operations in the conduct of Operations ENDURING FREEDOM and IRAQI FREEDOM. He coordinated to near completion the development of the irregular warfare execution roadmap and had a significant role in coordinating interagency partners' roles in counterterrorism operations around the world.

Winns' passionate commitment to the welfare and readiness of soldiers, sailors, airmen, and Marines made lasting contributions to national security and the GWOT.[168]

Vice Adm. Winns, the Naval Inspector General, voices his thoughts on the type of person who should join the Navy.

navy.com

Naval Inspector General

Admiral Winns' innovative leadership and comprehensive vision led the Office of the Naval Inspector General to unprecedented levels of efficiency and transparency. He personally briefed thousands of senior naval leaders on ethics and personal conduct. His dynamic engagement firmly established the Office of the Naval Inspector General as the conscience of the Navy. Admiral Winns improved visibility, teamwork, and cooperation and standardized inspection processes across the Navy enterprise.[169]

Rear Admiral Victor G. Guillory

Background

Victor Guillory was raised in New Orleans, Louisiana, in the Lower Ninth Ward—the district that was almost entirely destroyed during Hurricane Katrina. His mother passed away giving birth to him, so his grandmother raised him. That lady, who possessed a fifth-grade education, worked as a domestic in the area. While doing this work she became determined to provide her grandson the kind of lifestyle enjoyed by the individuals she served. She was a very hardworking woman, and she instilled character and a solid work ethic in him from an early age. She was also a huge proponent of doing the right thing—especially when no one else was watching.

Victor's grandmother ensured that he was protected from racism, and it was because of her hard work and oversight that he was able to become one of the first African Americans to graduate from one of the elite Catholic boarding schools in the area. While in this school, he enrolled in JROTC. This had a huge influence on his life, as the discipline and standards of the organization were similar to those he would experience later at USNA.

After graduating from high school, Guillory attended several small colleges in the area, but his great opportunity came when he was accepted, unexpectedly, to NAPS. Initially, Guillory had applied to the Air Force Academy, influenced by his JROTC instructor, a Master Sergeant Hyde; but the academies shared the candidate pool, and the

Navy offered him the position at NAPS. While attending NAPS, he became fast friends with Melvin Williams Jr., a future Navy vice admiral.

Guillory was very fortunate to experience a great deal of inclusion and team building during his junior officer years. An early CO, a Captain Myers, made it clear that Guillory would be judged on his performance, not his race. During these years, Guillory most often encountered awesome leaders who went beyond the call of duty to mentor him and to assist with his career.[170]

Significant Operational, Policy, and Technical Contributions

Tactical Action Officer, USS Vincennes *(CG 49)*

Lieutenant Commander Guillory displayed heroic achievement while stationed aboard this vessel, as demonstrated during the course of the surface engagement between *Vincennes* and an Iranian patrol craft in the Strait of Hormuz on July 3, 1988. He directed the maneuvering of *Vincennes* and USS *Elmer Montgomery* (FF 1082) at various courses and speeds to present the smallest possible profiles. As a result, the two ships under his tactical guidance, although subjected to intense hostile fire from five heavily armed patrol craft, received no structural damage; there were no personnel injuries; and all the attacking craft were sunk. Lieutenant Commander Guillory's ability to maintain his poise and confidence under direct fire contributed directly to the calm and professional atmosphere that reigned throughout the combat information center.[171] His experiences during this battle enabled Lieutenant Commander Guillory to understand how much pressure the Navy exerted on its commanding officers—and how much confidence it placed in them.

Commanding Officer, USS Lake Champlain *(CG 57)*

Captain Guillory's clear vision and sheer determination were demonstrated when *Lake Champlain* swept every departmental "E" for excellence, and in calendar year 2000 his command earned the Battle Efficiency Award and the Spokane Trophy for Combat Systems Excellence.

Guillory's firm and disciplined yet caring approach to command created an environment that motivated his sailors to embrace his goals and visions while reaffirming their commitment to the Navy's core values. By his leadership, the command won the calendar year 2000 CINC, U.S. Pacific Fleet Retention Excellence Award.[172]

Director, Surface Warfare Division, Staff of Deputy CNO

Admiral Guillory brilliantly spearheaded efforts to meet fleet and combatant command requirements for current and future surface combatants to close critical war-fighting gaps. His unwavering leadership and dedication extended the service life of more than seventy-five warships through the Aegis cruiser and destroyer modernization programs, and he developed future ship programs to unprecedented levels of maturity. Using extraordinary vision, he oversaw the Navy's newest combatant, the littoral combat ship, and paved the path for the addition of up to twenty ballistic missile defense-capable ships to the fleet by 2016.[173]

Commander, U.S. Naval Forces Southern Command and Commander, U.S. Fourth Fleet

Admiral Guillory singularly led USNAVSO and Fourth Fleet with charismatic leadership and skillful diplomacy, cultivating essential relationships with the military and political leaders of Latin American and Caribbean nations and establishing a firm foundation of trust. In addition, immediately following the devastating earthquake in Haiti in January 2010, Admiral Guillory established and sustained a joint seabasing force comprised of seventeen ships, eighty-nine aircraft, and over 15,000 sailors and Marines during Operation UNIFIED RESPONSE. By Admiral Guillory's demonstration of extraordinary leadership during UNIFIED RESPONSE and his orchestration of numerous staff process improvements, USNAVSO became the component of choice to respond to contingencies in USSOUTHCOM's area of responsibility.[174]

Rear Admiral Arthur J. Johnson

Background

Rear Admiral Arthur J. Johnson is a native of Burlington, Vermont. He graduated from USNA in May 1979 with a Bachelor of Science degree in international security affairs, with a focus on U.S. business and government relationships and third-world politics. Later he was a member of the Millennium Class at the National War College in Washington, DC.

Johnson attended flight training in Pensacola, Florida, and earned his wings as a naval aviator in February 1981. He deployed extensively throughout the Arabian Gulf, the Indian Ocean, and the Pacific region. A very capable mariner, he earned Third Fleet's Shiphandler of the Year honors in 1990 while serving aboard *Carl Vinson*.[175]

Significant Operational, Policy, and Technical Contributions

Action Officer, Strategy and Concepts Branch, Deputy CNO

Commander Johnson demonstrated exceptional leadership and insightful policy positions and solutions for several of the most critical long-term Navy and national defense issues. He distinguished himself in his role as a principal architect of the Navy's Latin

America strategic vision for the twenty-first century. His direct efforts laid the strategic foundation for sustaining an optimum naval presence in the region following the transition in control over the Panama Canal to the government of Panama in 1999. He was the Navy staff expert on peace operations and MOOTW. His insights and exhaustive research helped articulate the value of naval forces operating forward to support the important tenets of national security strategy.[176]

Executive Officer for Commander, Patrol and Reconnaissance Forces Eastern Atlantic

Commander Johnson's presence and watchful guidance provided unique undersea warfare expertise. He was directly responsible for the improved readiness of flight crews as he meticulously planned and executed warfare exercises that served as the standard for future undersea exercises. He was the driving force behind implementation of real-world submarine prosecutions that maintained U.S. Navy prominence in ASW.[177]

Commander, Patrol and Reconnaissance Wing 5

Captain Johnson's visionary efforts led the way in revitalizing community research-and-development efforts to incorporate commercial, off-the-shelf, leading-edge technology into unit infrastructures rapidly. His superb effort resulted in increased community war-fighting expertise and battle group interoperability. His superb leadership of over 1,400 personnel and his expert management of thirty-six P-3C aircraft ensured a ready inventory of mission-capable aircraft and combat-ready aircrews to support unified commanders in three frontline areas of operation. His insight and vision ensured that numerous technological advances were accomplished on time and within budget.[178]

Rear Admiral Earl L. Gay

Background

Earl Gay was born and reared in the Atlanta, Georgia, area; he was the youngest of three children. He was inspired to join the military by his heritage, as he came from a family of patriots: his great-grandfather served in World War II; his uncles served in various wars; and Gay's father-in-law fought alongside his brother in the Korean War, with both receiving Bronze Stars. Serving in the military was in Earl's blood, and he felt an obligation to honor the legacy of those who had gone before him.

Earl's father, a laborer, originally left school after the fifth grade, but later returned to the classroom to complete his GED. His mother, a high school graduate, eventually retired from General Motors. His family members were dedicated to hard work, and later he credited their determination with providing him a great foundation on which to build.

Gay eventually went to USNA, and after receiving his commission he entered the aviation community. During his junior officer tour, he worked extra hard to qualify early and maintain a competitive edge.

Gay did experience incidents in which race was a factor. On one occasion, while functioning as aircraft commander, he flew through a very bad storm to deliver a critical part to the ship. After landing he turned the aircraft over to the copilot and left to deliver the part. The XO of the ship was on the hangar deck to meet him, and when the two shook hands the XO said, "Tell the pilot that was an excellent landing!" Lieutenant Gay replied, "Sir, I AM the pilot." This instance did not really bother Gay; instead of getting upset, he focused on continuing to perform to the best of his ability. There were a number of other instances in which he was mistaken for a CPO, but he never let this bother him either.

Gay's participation in Operation DESERT STORM was extensive, as he was CO of USS *Belleau Wood* (LHA 3) when its Harrier jets flew combat sorties into Iraq. During this CO tour, he had to expedite training cycles several times to ensure Marines could be in Iraq prior to critical, upcoming Iraqi elections.

Once, while transporting Marines through the Strait of Hormuz, his ship's fueling state became very low—fuel was needed immediately. His team coordinated with a supply ship to receive fuel and other valuable services. But just as the supply vessel was pulling alongside, he received an order to provide close air support to troops on the ground in Iraq. So he had to multitask, successfully conducting underway replenishment and combat flight operations into Iraq simultaneously—one of his proudest accomplishments.[179]

Significant Operational, Policy, and Technical Contributions

Commanding Officer, Helicopter Antisubmarine Squadron Light 43

Commander Gay brought the "Battle Cats" to the forefront of tactical development and performance in the SH-60B Light Airborne Multi-Purpose System community. His visionary leadership and commitment to excellence successfully prepared and deployed the first SH-60B armed helicopters and conducted the first fleet Penguin-missile war shot firing. He also initiated the first operational evaluation for the night vision goggle head-up display system. His exceptional professionalism was further recognized when the Battle Cats were awarded the Lockheed-Martin Maintenance Excellence Award in 1996 and 1997 as well as the CNO Safety Award in 1996.[180]

Commandant, Naval District Washington

By articulating clear priorities, Rear Admiral Gay inspired a culture of top-notch management and customer service in the execution of more than one billion dollars' worth of full-spectrum base operating support within an environment of austerity and constrained manpower resources. Despite the systematic reduction of overtime expenditures by 10 percent, his exceptional leadership resulted in the public-private construction of nearly 300 homes; the renovation of 400 bachelor housing units; and the identification of approximately 174,000 square feet of the installation's footprint for reduction. During Gay's tenure, volunteerism soared and NDW personnel donated two million dollars to community projects.[181]

Commander, Expeditionary Strike Group 3

Rear Admiral Gay dynamically led twenty-four subordinate commands: four amphibious squadrons, twelve warships, and eight naval support elements. He displayed extraordinary vision and keen insight, as evidenced by Expeditionary Strike Group 3 ships earning the "Fit for Sustained Combat Operations" designation during inspections, including attainment of the highest score any LSD had achieved in recent history.

Gay also demonstrated uncommon leadership skills in ensuring that the first contact trials of USS *Makin Island* and USS *Green Bay* were highly successful, even though
each confronted myriad challenges associated with new construction. His foresight and
dynamic direction during exercises DAWN BLITZ 2010, IRON FIST 2011, and PACIFIC
HORIZON 2011 reinvigorated his team's ability to integrate and conduct large-scale
amphibious operations.[182]

Rear Admiral Kelvin N. Dixon

Background

Kelvin Dixon was born and raised in Tampa, Florida. His mother was a great inspiration to him and a great influence in his life, especially in promoting higher education. As an adolescent, he informed his parents that he wanted to become an engineer so he could drive a train someday—and a couple of decades later he graduated from Prairie View A&M University with a degree in mechanical engineering, with honors (one of three African American flag officers who graduated from Prairie View A&M University).

On admittance to Prairie View, he was required to enroll in either the Army or Navy ROTC program; he chose the Navy. He thoroughly enjoyed the program and ended up as Prairie View's battalion commander. He also experienced tragedy during this time: his father died in 1977, during Kelvin's freshman year of college. Kelvin's mentor at the time, Lieutenant Frank Jackson, who later became mayor of the city of Prairie View, took him under his wing. Jackson guided Kelvin throughout his time in NROTC, and continued as a wonderful mentor throughout his naval career.

As a new ensign, Kelvin found it quite a challenge to adjust, leaving a segregated community to live and work surrounded by individuals from different backgrounds. Understanding the Navy vernacular and adjusting to shipboard life also constituted challenges. However, he had mentors who reached out and guided him throughout his career. His early career aspirations were to make commander and thus to wear "scrambled eggs" (signifying relatively high rank) on his cover [hat], but he went on to accomplish significantly more—Admiral Dixon completed nine CO tours. Admiral Dixon's sterling career afforded him the joy of exercising leadership. Reaching back to help all sailors reach their full potential was, and still is, a premier goal for him.[183]

Significant Operational, Policy, and Technical Contributions

Commanding Officer, Naval Reserve, Naval Beach Group 2 (NBG-2), Detachment 206

Commander Dixon's exceptional ability to guide and motivate his crew empowered it to excel operationally and meet all tasked assignments. He maintained his unit in a poised, combat-ready status and deployed nine detachments in support of exercises DELMAR 1999 and DELMAR 2000, two major Maritime Prepositioning Force exercises in Norfolk, Virginia. In fulfilling his responsibility for the naval support element, he executed highly efficient and safe exercises with over 150 reservists as well as active-duty personnel, and landing craft-mechanized, landing craft-utility, landing craft-air cushion, and other beach-party equipment. During his tour, NBG-2 Detachment 206 provided over 6000 hours of support to Commander, Amphibious Group 2 and sustained unit readiness at 96 percent.[184]

Commanding Officer, Navy Reserve Commander, U.S. Navy Forces Central Command Bahrain, Detachment 109

During all phases of Operations ENDURING FREEDOM and IRAQI FREEDOM and the GWOT, Captain Dixon's unit achieved an extraordinary level of mission accomplishment and readiness in direct support of Commander, U.S. Navy Forces Central Command, guiding his unit to maintain mission requirements at or near 100 percent. With one third of his unit mobilized, including himself, his innovative leadership used a bottom-up approach; reviewing each assigned billet enabled optimization of all resources available for future operational support.[185]

Commanding Officer, Naval Reserve Detachment 606, Naval Surface Fleet, U.S. Atlantic Fleet

Captain Dixon's business acumen and innovative leadership created the first-ever afloat cultural workshop program in the surface enterprises, a waterfront weekend fleet orientation program, the supply corps basic qualification course, and a sea-mentoring program for reserve personnel. He spearheaded relief efforts during Hurricane Katrina that focused on unaccounted-for active-component personnel and their families. He set high standards for unit training and readiness, which resulted in the successful mobilization of personnel to Iraq and Afghanistan in support of the GWOT.

Dixon led a meticulous review of critical and noncritical flexible hoses for amphibious ships, which reduced critical hose requirements by 30 percent, saving taxpayers over 1.2 million dollars. His leadership in providing oversight of his unit's reconciliation of depot-level repairable transactions recovered over 1.1 million dollars.[186]

Director, Iraq Training and Advisory Mission

While supporting Operations IRAQI FREEDOM and NEW DAWN, Admiral Dixon's outstanding leadership and ceaseless efforts resulted in major contributions to U.S. national security by training more than 3000 Iraqi navy and marine personnel in equipping and sustaining a fleet of more than fifty vessels. Additionally, his personal dedication to improving Iraqi C2, fostering regional partnerships, and coordinating 929 million dollars in foreign military sales transformed the Iraqi navy and marine forces into a capable maritime force, ready to protect Iraq's critical maritime oil infrastructure.[187]

Rear Admiral Sinclair Harris

Background

Sinclair Harris was raised in the Anacostia and Deanwood sections of Washington, DC, by a hardworking single mother who had served in the Army for a short period. Seeing her persistence and her skillful approach to human relations made a huge impact on his life—she taught him to treat people with dignity and respect.

Harris' first interaction with the Navy came when he read an *Ebony* magazine article that named Admiral Gravely one of the hundred most influential African Americans. This had a profound impact on him. Another early Navy interaction was an encounter with one of his mother's tenants, who worked at the Washington Navy Yard. This gentleman's stories about his Navy adventures intrigued the young Harris, and he considered joining right away.

In 1977, after receiving the requisite scores on the SAT exam, Sinclair applied for admission to USNA, but was turned down. He decided to enlist; however, his uncle, a retired Air Force senior master technical sergeant, encouraged him to attend college first. Harris eventually attained his degree from James Madison University. After working for a few years, he wanted to see the world, so he walked into a recruiter's office, joined the Navy, and reported to OCS.[188]

Significant, Operational, Policy, and Technical Contributions

Commanding Officer, USS Comstock *(LSD 45)*

Commander Harris transported the first wave of Marines to Iraq in support of Operation ENDURING FREEDOM.[189]

Warfighting Campaign Analysis Branch Head, Staff of the Deputy CNO

Captain Harris provided the ability to view across warfare, support, and readiness areas to determine future operational and capability risks inherent in investment options for the Navy's hundred-billion-dollar program. He significantly advanced Navy strategic and programmatic interests within the joint staff and the office of the Secretary of Defense. A brilliant analyst, he innovatively conceptualized and initiated efforts to model difficult and complex phenomena that enabled capability sponsors to quantify better the impact of investment in future Navy systems in a joint war fight. His accomplishments over a broad range of war-fighting capability and readiness issues laid important and significant groundwork for transformation of the service into a twenty-first-century Navy.[190]

Commander, Amphibious Squadron 4 (PHIBRON 4) and the Iwo Jima *Strike Group*

Captain Harris served as commodore of PHIBRON 4, and as the deputy Sea Echelon commander was a key leader in the response to Hurricanes Katrina and Rita. His span of control covered the Gulf Coast and the Mississippi River; his command provided support to those impacted by the disaster and first responders. Later in this tour, Commodore Harris led his forces in the safe evacuation of nearly fifteen thousand people from Lebanon during fighting between Israel and Hezbollah.

Chief, Security Assistance Division, Deputy Directorate for Global Security Affairs, the Joint Staff

Captain Harris was the primary point of contact for the CJCS for all policies related to building partnership capacity and exceptions to national disclosure. Tirelessly working the interagency process, he consistently advanced Building Partnership Capacity (BPC) initiatives through DoD, where they became two of the top three legislative priorities. Captain Harris developed an aggressive congressional outreach program that helped overcome broad opposition to the DoD BPC authorities. As the Joint Staff senior representative, Captain Harris played a crucial role in DoD's Iraq Foreign Military Sales Task Force. His guidance and decisive inputs were critical to streamlining the sales and distribution process significantly and helped expedite the equipping of Iraq's security forces. His superior leadership led to the development and funding of a BPC operational picture system for the Joint Staff, combatant commanders, and the services that synchronized and streamlined real-time partnership efforts worldwide.[191]

Deputy Director and Director, Expeditionary Warfare Division

Admiral Harris' extraordinary vision and innovative leadership enabled the Expeditionary Warfare Division to employ the Surface Warfare and Naval Expeditionary Combat Enterprises to increase support to current combat operations while posturing expeditionary forces for lasting success. His sage oversight positively impacted the wide portfolio of expeditionary warfare programs covering over twenty-two billion dollars in appropriations across the Future Years Defense Plan. He recognized the increasing range of mission areas inherent to the Navy's expeditionary forces, fostered strong interagency relationships, and established clear lines of communication among the services. This resulted in a balanced strategy for expeditionary warfare in Program Object Memorandum 2010 and Program Review 2011. His astute judgment and creativity served as the foundation for fiscally sound decisions for expeditionary warfare programs and requirements to preserve the relevance and integrity of naval expeditionary warfare.[192]

Commander, Expeditionary Strike Group 5

Admiral Harris was directly and positively responsible for the successful establishment of expeditionary Strike Group 5. He displayed visionary leadership and operational brilliance in directing U.S. Naval Forces CENTCOM TFs 51, 52, 55, and 59, comprising more than twenty ships, thirty-nine aircraft, and 4,500 sailors and Marines. His command presence and proactive role in fifty key leader engagements and forty-one theater security cooperation events throughout the region were instrumental in the execution of sixteen bilateral exercises in support of persistent security force assistance to the combatant commanders.[193]

Director, Navy Future Concepts for the Deputy CNO

Admiral Harris' wise judgment and dynamic direction led to his comprehensive grasp of national and international military insights that were of incalculable value to the Secretary of Defense and the Department of the Navy. He played a significant role in formulating and developing plans and technologies to support worldwide U.S. security objectives during a period of unprecedented political turbulence and combat operations. Admiral Harris' innovative leadership led the Navy's efforts through outreach in strategic and programmatic decision-making forums that defined DoD and national policies regarding the air-sea battle concept and the mainstream Navy's efforts to confront irregular challenges. He was also the driving force behind sustaining a spiraled approach to developing new technologies and rapidly fielding these technologies to support combatant command warfighters directly.[194]

Commander, U.S. Fourth Fleet and Naval Forces Southern Command

By his constant engagement and collaboration, Admiral Harris inspired greater cooperation between the U.S. Navy and the various national maritime forces of Central America, South America, and the Caribbean. Leadership of PANAMAX 2012 highlighted his tour as commander, U.S. Fourth Fleet and UNITAS 2012, during which he led multinational coalitions in a wide variety of at-sea exercises.

Vice Director for Operations, Joint Chiefs of Staff (VDJ3)

Admiral Harris's final assignment was as Vice Director for Operations on the staff of the Chairman of the Joint Chiefs of Staff. From deploying forces to combat violent extremists to responding to natural disasters, Admiral Harris was a key contributor to the planning and execution of global operations by the United States. He was well known within the Office of the Secretary of Defense and the National Security Council for decisive and positive results when addressing the most difficult tasks.

Rear Admiral Norman R. Hayes

Background

Norman Hayes was born in Chicago, Illinois. He did not spend much time with his father, so his mother influenced him heavily. She was a very strong, capable woman who personified perseverance and determination. She was not afraid to change locations if new opportunities presented themselves; therefore, while a youngster, Norman moved extensively, living in ten states and attending twenty-four schools, including seven high schools. His mother enforced strong education standards on her children, so at an early age he understood that making excellent grades in school was mandatory.

Throughout high school Norman thought about becoming a part of the military, but did not act on the idea until later. After graduating from Indiana University, he worked in the civilian sector, but did not find it fulfilling. Hayes observed his civilian counterparts exhibiting unfairness, and he thought he would receive a fairer assessment of his abilities if he joined the military. He viewed the military as a meritocracy in which individuals were judged on their abilities, not on preconceived notions derived from their race or anything else. After coming to this conclusion, he walked directly into the recruiter's office, took the entrance exam, and was on his way to becoming a naval officer. He initially wanted to fly jets for the Navy; however, his vision did not allow participation in the aviation community. But having made a high entrance exam score, he was offered a position in Naval Intelligence.

After fifteen months of contemplating whether he should accept the Navy's offer, Hayes finally decided to do so. He completed OCS, then was admitted into the Naval Intelligence Corps. Along the way, he struggled with the swimming portion of his training but persevered. He was very comfortable assimilating into the military environment because he was well traveled and had experienced many cultures while traveling the country with his mother.

As a lieutenant in 1989, Hayes was the first African American naval officer to work in the front office of what was then the Department of Naval Intelligence, where he became the deputy executive assistant to the director of intelligence.[195]

Significant Operational, Policy, and Technical Contributions

Executive Officer, Directorate of Intelligence and Chief, Analysis Division, Joint Intelligence Center, U.S. Special Operations Command

Commander Hayes displayed innovative leadership in his conceptualization of two prototype products that supported U.S. Special Operations Command Plan 0400. This plan forged ties with the command's special-mission units and helped promote throughout DoD the analytical and mission-support capabilities of the Special Operations Command Joint Intelligence Center.

Hayes planned, established, and executed an extensive analyst training program that increased analytical depth and breadth to account for shortages in manpower and experience. He also superbly managed the integration of over seventy-five reserve personnel into the Analysis Division structure, a very effective program that not only supported the mission but developed critical thinkers in the Intelligence Community.[196]

Intelligence Officer, USS Abraham Lincoln (CVN 72)

Commander Hayes was the driving force behind the restructuring of the carrier intelligence center. His efforts resulted in superior intelligence support to the battle group warfare commander and staffs while deployed to the Arabian Gulf. He fostered responsibility at the most junior level and produced an atmosphere conducive to individual excellence. As the project manager for the first-ever installation of the Naval Fires Network on a nuclear aircraft carrier, Hayes' timely coordination ensured the smooth and effective installation of a twenty-seven-million-dollar system. His hands-on approach significantly contributed to the exceptionally high operational readiness, morale, and retention within the carrier intelligence center and was a critical element in the ship's receipt of the 2001 Arleigh Burke Award.[197]

Commanding Officer, Center for Naval Intelligence and Navy and Marine Corps Intelligence Training Center

Rear Admiral Hayes' performance during this tour was very inspirational. Despite a dramatic expansion of training requirements resulting in a 100 percent increase in student throughput, he remained steadfastly focused on the sailors and the curriculum. He not only managed twenty-nine courses with over 5,600 students, with no additional personnel and without degradation in training quality, but he simultaneously reduced attrition rates.

To strengthen the Intelligence Community by promoting diversity, he acted as ambassador for the Navy and Naval Intelligence in developing a partnership between the Center for Naval Intelligence and Norfolk State University.[198]

Rear Admiral Vincent L. Griffith

Background

Vincent Griffith was reared on a farm in a small town in Georgia. His father was a Baptist minister, a strict disciplinarian, and his mother was a homemaker. Vincent was one of four siblings, and was taught early on that maintaining one's integrity, practicing a work ethic, and having a positive attitude would make life much easier. His parents taught him self-reliance.

Vincent attended Berry College, a private school that boasts of having over 80 percent of its students work on campus, with an emphasis on peer development and giving back to the community. During his junior year, he had an internship with the Sears Corporation, which caused him to consider a career in business. After consulting with his supervisors at Sears, he decided that the Navy was his best option because he could pursue a "business" career—the Supply Corps would be his Navy community of choice—while giving back to the community simultaneously.

When Griffith reported to his first command, his CO immediately encouraged him to reach for the stars. He learned early on that working longer and smarter now would pay big dividends in the future.

An interesting experience in Charleston, South Carolina, taught him that people are busy, and they are interested in folks they know; so what might be perceived as discrimination could be only a misunderstanding. This realization led to his goal of trying to meet at least two people at any event he attends. Admiral Griffith is a strong advocate of mentoring and ensuring that everyone feels welcome in his surroundings.[199]

Significant Operational, Policy, and Technical Contributions

Deputy Force Supply Officer, Commander Naval Air Force

Commander Griffith's keen insight and forward thinking were key components of the overall superior performance that COMNAVAIRPAC Force Supply demonstrated. Immediately following the attacks of September 11th, Commander Griffith implemented a broad array of initiatives to support Operation ENDURING FREEDOM aggressively. Owing to his direct efforts, USS *Carl Vinson* (CVN 70), USS *Kitty Hawk* (CV 63), and USS *John C. Stennis* (CVN 74) were able to sustain and execute the high wartime operational tempos. He innovatively created the Requirements Branch to insert the fleet fully into the aviation spares requirement process, which provided a platform to influence the budget cycle to ensure critical fleet requirements were met. In addition, by instituting a COMNAVAIRPAC/COMNAVAIRLANT alignment, he created a synergetic organization that facilitated the exercise of a single voice for naval aviation supply logistics policy to engage fleet customers fully. This resulted in a unified Naval Air Force that supported transformational technologies, innovative concepts, and system enhancement.[200]

Assistant Chief of Staff for Force Supply, Commander Naval Air Forces

Captain Griffith provided strategic leadership and vision through his active involvement in all naval aviation enterprise (NAE) readiness-improvement forums, including those dealing with career readiness and maintenance and supply chain management, as well as the airspeed executive steering committee. He created efficient operational opportunities that achieved program manpower and budget savings in support of the tactical objectives of the NAE strategic management plan. He also implemented aviation support execution guidance that saved 477 million dollars in flying-hour program funding and set policy and guidance for twenty-six ashore aviation activities, ten type wings, and twelve aircraft carriers, with a total operating budget and inventory of four and twelve billion dollars, respectively. He was instrumental in the successful standup of the EA-18G and the inaugural combat deployment of the MV-22 to Al Asad, Iraq, in support of Operations IRAQI FREEDOM and ENDURING FREEDOM.

Captain Griffith's innovative support plan resulted in over 3,600 flight hours and an 80 percent mission-completion rate. He directed advance preparations to support integration of the Joint Strike Fighter (F-35) into aircraft carrier operations, providing a focused collaboration of optimized logistics support and cost-wise readiness.

Additionally, Captain Griffith established extensive and effective outreach relationships that projected the NAE as a diversity partner within the Navy. He demonstrated that the Navy was an employer of choice, resulting in the sponsorship of twelve minority scholars into the officer-accession pipeline as future aviators—the highest contribution by any enterprise.[201]

Commander, Defense Logistics Agency

Admiral Griffith's exceptional leadership, devotion to excellence, and dedication led DLA to accomplish more than 900 value engineering projects in FY 2009 and FY 2010. These projects focused on reliability improvements, reverse engineering, source development, and price reductions. He creatively implemented disciplined production control across the entire DLA aviation supply chain. He superbly led an organization responsible for all support pertaining to aviation spares to military services, theater commanders, international coalition partners, weapon systems program managers, and industrial sites.[202]

Director, Fleet Ordnance and Supply

Admiral Griffith's exceptional leadership and extraordinary logistics expertise drove significant changes in numerous Navy logistics and ordnance processes that resulted in significant improvements in fleet readiness. As the driving force in the rapid analysis and effective correction of a long-standing shortfall in shipboard spares, his direct efforts reversed a five-year negative trend in supply effectiveness measures. His personal leadership in the development and implementation of enhanced logistics support for Aegis/ballistic-missile defense systems yielded rapid and dramatic improvements in the performance and operational availability of these critical weapon systems.

Griffith's direction of a cross-functional team from echelon 1 and 2 commands produced a more rational and effective ordnance allocation process that increased the efficiency of ship ordnance loading and the availability of training ordnance, increasing fleet readiness. He collaborated with system commands to position critical spares forward in direct support of deployed units; for instance, patrol coastal craft supply achieved 100 percent readiness only six months after his process changes were implemented. His determined leadership to address and resolve difficult problems across the Navy and DoD supply chains yielded positive results and laid the foundation for sustained, long-term improvement in operational readiness.[203]

Admiral Michelle Howard

Background

Michelle Howard was born in Aurora, Colorado. She was one of four siblings and was taught the value of education, self-respect, perseverance, justice, and equality at an early age. Providing an environment that fostered these principles was a priority for her parents. Howard inherited a legacy of perseverance: her father quit school as an adolescent to help support his family by shining shoes. At seventeen he joined the Air Force, and eventually obtained his GED; he retired when she was twelve years old.[204]

Michelle learned early that perseverance was a trait she would need to overcome obstacles. When she was five years old, someone used a racial slur when speaking to her. She ran home and told her father, but did not get the reaction she expected. "My father picked me up and shook me," says Howard. "He shook me and he said, 'You get used to it, little girl. You've got to toughen up. That's just the way it is.'"[205] She would need this type of perseverance to get through USNA and the challenging career ahead, which included being the first woman to command a warship.

As a youngster, Howard saw a documentary on television that mentioned the federal service academies. When she inquired, she discovered they were not open to women. But her mother insisted, "If the law is not changed by the time you apply, we will sue the government and set a precedent." Fortunately, the law changed when she was sixteen, and she applied to USNA when she was eighteen. She chose the Naval Academy because her research indicated the Navy offered more options for women than the other services. Six African American women graduated from the Academy in her class of 1982.

During her time at USNA, the Combat Exclusion Law—legislation passed after World War II that prevented women from serving in combat roles—essentially restricted the ships on which women could serve to hospital ships. During her first class midshipman summer cruise, she and her female colleagues were not permitted to board a mine-sweeper, even though they had orders to do so. The ship had been unaware that women were en route, and refused to accept the female midshipmen aboard, justifying this by a lack of prepared accommodations.

Admiral Howard would eventually contribute to a series of firsts for African Americans and women, including being the first African American woman to command a Navy ship, attain two stars in the Navy, and attain three- and four-star status in any U.S. armed service. Howard considers mentorship the catalyst that enabled her to capitalize on opportunities and prepare her for future assignments; she herself currently mentors many junior and senior officers.

Admiral Howard's innovative leadership played a significant role in shaping the Navy's diversity policy to allow women to serve in various roles after the Combat Exclusion Law was repealed. She was the lead action officer working with a host of other women to design the Navy's policy for inclusion of women in various combat roles.[206] One of the guiding principles required that DoD be aligned across the services, so when a particular field was made available to Navy women, the other services had to offer it to their female troops as well.

Significant Operational, Policy, and Technical Contributions

Main Engine Officer, USS Lexington *(AVT 16)*

Lieutenant Howard's demonstration of inspirational leadership and managerial skills was unprecedented. She motivated her division to seek greater levels of responsibility actively, which elevated the division to unprecedented standards in maintenance, repair, and training. Her direct involvement contributed to USS *Lexington*'s high state of mission readiness and proved to be the key to the ship passing its first operational propulsion plant examination in recent history.[207]

Chief Engineer, USS Mount Hood *(AE 29)*

Words such as *meticulous, flawless,* and *unsurpassed skills* were commonly used when describing Lieutenant Howard's ability to get things done as engineering officer on this vessel. During an operational propulsion plant examination, Lieutenant Howard flaw-lessly coordinated the presentation of numerous simultaneous evolutions and program reviews. Her long-term commitment to daily high standards in administration, mate-rial readiness, cleanliness, and plant operations enabled the engineering department to execute this particular inspection with minimum preparation. Her meticulous attention to detail significantly contributed to success in this examination.

Lieutenant Howard maintained an exceptional continuum of readiness throughout her department as she met every challenge and commitment placed before her, includ-ing two engineering mobile training team visits and an operational propulsion plant examination executed in an unprecedented thirty-six hours without significant deficiencies. Under her astute leadership and creativity, USS *Mount Hood*'s engineering plant steamed continuously for 160 days during Operations DESERT SHIELD and DESERT STORM, while still performing significant propulsion plant maintenance. Her attention to detail and innovation were manifested in a superb type commander boiler inspection and the successful completion of the security alarm maintenance phase of a zero-discrepancy, short-notice Navy technical proficiency inspection.[208]

Commanding Officer, USS Rushmore *(LSD 47)*

In commanding the Navy's only "smart" amphibious platform at the time, Commander Howard demonstrated exceptional leadership and creativity in leading the ship through arduous western Pacific and Arabian Gulf deployments. During deployment exercises IRON MAGIC '99 and RED REEF '10, *Rushmore* demonstrated a level of coalition interoperability not matched since Operation DESERT STORM in embarking elements of the Marines and transporting them over 120 miles for launching during the exercises. As CO of the first and only Navy smart ship to complete a six-month deployment, Commander Howard oversaw the testing and evaluation of newly installed commercial off-the-shelf technologies, while successfully meeting all assigned missions.[209]

Commander, Amphibious Squadron 7

Captain Howard demonstrated exceptional leadership and tactical vision, transforming her command into a dynamic and lethal maritime force that executed extensive operations throughout the volatile and high-threat environment of the Arabian Gulf in support of Operations ENDURING FREEDOM and IRAQI FREEDOM. As the maritime security operations warfare commander for TF 58, she developed and implemented a brilliant security plan for the protection of the Al Basra and Kawar Al Amaya oil terminals by coalition forces whose efforts ensured the defense of those vital assets, aiding tremendously Iraq's political and economic stability. She led her squadron as it conducted HADR missions, including providing over twenty-one million pounds of relief supplies to the victims of the devastating tsunami off the coasts of Indonesia and Sri Lanka during Operation UNIFIED ASSISTANCE.[210]

Commander, Expeditionary Strike Group 2

Rear Admiral Howard's leadership produced unprecedented levels of success. She commanded one multinational and three U.S. task forces, involving planning and execution responsibilities that spanned the spectrum of contingency response to major combat operations. Her tactical vision was critical to executing the time-sensitive mission that rescued Captain Richard Phillips, a civilian mariner held captive by Somali pirates. Her efforts reinvigorated the strike group's efforts to ensure the combat readiness of amphibious ships and equipment. This mission was highly visible, and had it not been successful there might have been far-reaching and possibly negative consequences for the United States and its partners abroad. However, Rear Admiral Howard's Navy team performed this task flawlessly.[211]

"Men have the luxury of being average. When you walk in as a woman, that assumption does not come with you."—Michelle Howard, former commanding officer, USS *Rushmore*

Rear Admiral Charles K. Carodine

Background

Charles Carodine was born in Huntsville, Alabama. His father died when he was very young, so his mother and a caring stepfather raised him. Both of his parents were college educated and his stepfather, a former Army member, put himself through school and became a mathematician who designed computer models for military weaponry. Because of his stepfather's support and encouragement, Charles and the other children of the Carodine household excelled in mathematics, science, and engineering concepts.

Huntsville was home to a portion of the space program, and through the years individuals such as Alan Shepard, one of the original Mercury Seven astronauts, visited the community and spoke to youth groups. This educational experience influenced the young Carodine (from the time he was eight years old) to consider attending USNA. He held fast to that dream and applied to the Academy during his senior year of high school. When he did not receive correspondence from the Navy, he accepted a position in the U.S. Air Force Academy Preparatory School. This was a mistake, as he did not enjoy the preparatory school at all, so he again applied to USNA and was accepted.

After graduation, Carodine experienced unique challenges while serving as a junior officer on his first ship. After the scheduled relief of his first CO, life aboard took a turn for the worse. He was the only African American on the ship, and his new CO treated him with much cruelty. The CO berated Carodine in front of his men and visitors, publicly humiliated him at every opportunity, and restricted him to the ship at least eight times.

On one occasion, Carodine left the ship to follow up on ship repair items. When he returned to the ship after about an hour, the petty officer of the watch told him a meeting was underway in the wardroom and that he should hurry to get there. (The crewmembers understood the scrutiny he was under, and many tried to assist him.) As soon as Carodine entered the wardroom, the captain closed the session—with a bit of a smirk. Once everyone cleared out, his best friend told him, "The captain was discussing how you have to treat and talk to the 'black troops'; then you walked in and he dismissed the meeting immediately."

The cruelty was so severe that Lieutenant Carodine eventually sought help from the base chaplain. Yet despite this horrible experience on his first ship, Carodine persevered. From that first CO, he chose to learn what *not* to do. After his initial sea tours, Carodine transitioned to the reserves. He is very grateful for the opportunities he received, and he firmly believes that for every person who tried to cause him harm in his career, several others went out of their way to offer assistance.[212]

Significant Operational, Policy, and Technical Contributions

Assistant Chief of Staff for Information Systems, Naval Reserve Readiness Command South, Fort Worth, Texas

Commander Carodine used superb professionalism, vision, and inspiring leadership to lead over 7000 Naval reservists across a five-state region. He demonstrated these qualities as the driving force behind and primary architect of the regional transition to the Navy and Marine Corps Intranet, creating a detailed listing of tasks and associated responsibilities. Using his extensive IT background, he developed and delivered several informative and articulate briefs to reserve center COs and REDCOM staff personnel to prepare them for this major transition.[213]

Commanding Officer, Expeditionary Port Unit 1112, Military Sealift Command

Captain Carodine's exceptional managerial and creative leadership skills were clearly demonstrated as he masterfully orchestrated the complete revitalization of an undermanned and undertrained unit into a fully mobilization-ready and mission-oriented expeditionary unit. Under his direct guidance, MSC reservists provided more than 10,000 man-hours of operational support worldwide to meet mission requirements. He devised a plan to analyze missions and manpower and codify training requirements. He identified key indicators of readiness, resulting in an increase in the unit's mobilization readiness level from C4 to C1.

Captain Carodine was the principal programmer and developer for the Web-based software prototype of the MSC Reserve Manning and Reporting System, which was a follow-on to his PC-based application for reporting the readiness of Military Sealift Reserve Units to both area commanders and headquarters.[214]

Deputy Commander, Navy Warfare Development Command

Admiral Carodine led his team with inspirational leadership and strategic vision, and skillfully executed his duties so as to increase the effectiveness and overall capability of the Navy's warfare-development efforts. He was the linchpin in an initiative to restructure the Navy's approach to using IT in maritime and counterpiracy operations, which is currently a component of the Navy Warfare Development Command's concept work in response to the 2012 CNO's Information Dominance Initiative.

Admiral Carodine developed a Navy Lessons Learned Information System Improvement Plan that meshed connections between the Joint Staff and Naval Warfare Systems Command, along with other Navy entities, to resolve Joint-Navy Lessons Learned Information System issues.

Admiral Carodine drove the organizational realignment initiative that integrated staff functions with joint and service objectives, which elevated command services and products to bridge operational and strategic gaps. He developed the first-ever cyber capabilities plan, offering Navy Warfare Development Command concepts, doctrine, experimentation, and modeling and simulation services to the Tenth Fleet, while establishing information operations range nodes in the Navy Continuous Training Environment suite to inject cyber activities into all future experiment and simulation events.[215]

Director, Navy Business Operations Office

Admiral Carodine distinguished himself by leading numerous initiatives to align resources optimally to deliver best business practices across the CNO staff and provider enterprise. He developed innovative strategies that fortified discipline in the validation of contracted support requirements. Through judicious approaches to contract-award procedures and accountability, he achieved savings in excess of forty-nine million dollars. His creativity was exemplified in his alignment of 240 separate logistics information technician systems across twenty-two budget support offices to form twenty-three programs of record that transparently integrated the Navy's complex network.

Admiral Carodine also played a leading role in transitioning the Navy Enterprise Resource Planning System to organic sustainment, which resulted in 57.6 million dollars in savings over the five-year defense plan.[216]

Rear Admiral Kevin D. Scott

Background

Kevin Scott's mother was reared in Portsmouth, Virginia, and was the salutatorian of her class. Because of the lack of opportunities in the South during this time, the family decided to relocate to New York. Kevin was born in Brooklyn, New York, in March 1960. After a time, his mother sent him to live with his grandparents in Alabama while she continued working in New York. His grandparents thus played a major role in his life, as did growing up in the segregated part of town.

But when Kevin's grandfather passed away in 1966, his mother, a single parent who had been supporting him on her salary as a housekeeper, was able to obtain better employment, and she reunited the family in New York soon thereafter. Although he was accustomed to the segregated South, he excelled in elementary school in New York, learning at an early age that diversity in any culture should be embraced. This experience continues to shape his decision-making process today.

Kevin's family eventually moved from Manhattan to the Bronx, and he enrolled in the Bronx High School of Science, an all-male and majority institution. His natural talent in leadership and academics allowed him to skip the ninth grade, and he finished high school with honors.

Scott always had been interested in flying. Nonetheless, upon entering college he decided to major in computer science, but he soon found that his heart was not in it. One day while riding a city bus, he saw in the back of a newspaper a photo of a Navy fighter pilot sitting in the cockpit of a fighter jet. He gave the bus driver the address listed in the ad, and the driver drove him there! He signed up for AROCS. However, after he had signed up, the program was canceled. At that point, he engaged in a heated debate with the recruiter over the prospect of not flying for the Navy; but a Navy lieutenant, hearing the raised voices, calmed the young Scott by asking him whether he could graduate from college in the summer, so they could get him into October's AOCS class. Scott ended up graduating early from college and began his career in naval aviation.

On the day Scott reported as an AOCS candidate, he encountered a Ku Klux Klan rally at the gate. Beyond that, his overall story is similar to those of several other African American flag officers, in that he was the first college graduate in his family, he had few mentors, the maritime environment was foreign, and workplace isolation was common. Consequently, it took great perseverance to get through the AOCS program; but failure was not an option. He credits his own hard work and perseverance and what mentoring he did receive for providing the opportunities that challenged him and sharpened his leadership skills.[217]

Significant Operational, Policy, and Technical Contributions

Commodore, Mine Countermeasures Squadron 1

Captain Scott's operational expertise and distinguished service significantly improved his squadron's battle readiness to new levels of operations and sustainability. Through his keen vision and inspiring commitment to combat readiness, he deployed his force to support exercises and significantly contributed to fleet engagement with western Pacific nations located in the Seventh and Third Fleet areas of operation.

Scott planned and executed tactical control of U.S. and allied mine countermeasures by air, surface, and underwater forces in twelve multinational mine countermeasure exercises that strengthened regional commitment throughout the Pacific. He commanded a task group of eight mine countermeasures ships and several aircraft that significantly contributed to maritime traffic navigation in the Gulf of Mexico.[218]

Director, Aviation Office Distribution Division

Captain Scott's dynamic leadership was critical to achieving and maintaining unsurpassed aviation officer fleet manning levels and readiness during a time of extraordinary economic turmoil, inventory shortages, and increasing manpower requirements in support of the GWOT. His direct efforts produced transformational changes to manning strategies and the career management of over 12,000 aviation officers; he surpassed mission priorities, which resulted in an unprecedented manpower effectiveness rating of 99 percent. Simultaneously, he met GWOT manpower requirements, including sustainment of a 300-person counter-improvised explosive device detachment.

Scott championed the expansion of the concept of specialty career paths to all unrestricted line communities to expand career opportunities for mid-grade officers with critical skill sets. Further, as the Naval Air Force diversity lead, he directed the development of a career milestone tracking tool that was instrumental in improving diversity in the naval aviation community.[219]

Director, Expeditionary Warfare Division

Admiral Scott's keen intellect and superb leadership ensured that surface warfare and naval expeditionary combat forces were best employed to plan, program, budget, and execute the recapitalization of expeditionary forces. While operating in an austere fiscal environment, his unsurpassed expertise resulted in a nineteen-billion-dollar expeditionary warfare program portfolio that fully supported combat operations, both ongoing and those postulated for the future. He established solid lines of communications and developed relationships throughout DoD that fostered a cogent and a fiscally balanced strategy for expeditionary warfare. His contributions provided more robust Navy expeditionary command initiatives that enhanced joint operations into the foreseeable future.[220]

Commander, Expeditionary Strike Group 2

Admiral Scott distinguished himself through his brilliant leadership of over 20,000 sailors and Marines stationed aboard sixteen ships and in three amphibious ready groups and eight deployable commands in the Atlantic and Mediterranean regions. Instilling in his commanders a warrior ethos and focusing them on unit and collective readiness, he guided his expeditionary strike group to distinctive success in support of Operations ODYSSEY DAWN and UNIFIED PROTECTOR with the Sixth, Fifth, and Fourth Fleets. He maintained his forces in the highest state of readiness and rendered lifesaving assistance to American citizens in the wake of Hurricane Irene. His creativity and innovation culminated in the flawless execution of BOLD ALLIGATOR 2012, the largest amphibious exercise in over a decade.[221]

Rear Admiral John W. Smith Jr.

Background

John Smith was born in the borough of Queens but was raised in Brooklyn, both in New York City. He was the oldest of six siblings. His parents were blue-collar workers who labored tirelessly to keep their children off the streets and out of trouble. John's sixth-grade math teacher ignited his interest in that subject and encouraged him to excel. As an adolescent, sports were an important part of his life that provided him with a healthy outlet in which to engage with friends. At an early age, he told his mother that he believed that to be successful he would have to leave Brooklyn.

After graduating from high school, John was admitted to South Carolina State College in Orangeburg. After graduating with an accounting degree, he returned to New York and worked in that field. After two years, he decided that he was not being fulfilled by working as an accountant. A chance encounter at his office with an Army major wearing his military uniform caused him to consider the opportunities the military could provide. The two men had a discussion, and the major ultimately succeeded in convincing him to join the military, which he did via AOCS.

Rear Admiral Smith has had many wonderful mentors during his life, but he also has learned from negative experiences as well. One particularly memorable experience occurred when he was thirteen years old. He was walking with friends through a neighborhood to go fishing when suddenly it started "raining rocks." The experience taught him to act quickly and decisively when confronted with adversity. Also, while serving on his first ship, his CO informed him that he would never become a CO. These seemingly negative experiences strengthened his resolve to push beyond any manmade barriers and excel.

Smith acknowledges that for every person who meant him harm, there were always four or five who supported him. Such an instance occurred when he was a sophomore at South Carolina State College. He was carrying a GPA of 3.4, but despite his strong academic performance, he found himself unable to register for classes—he was out of money. He took his transcript to the president's house and said, "I need help." The president gave him a signed note that allowed him to register for class and remain in college.[222]

Significant Operational, Policy, and Technical Contributions

Head, Aviation Commander Assignments, Naval Personnel Command

Commander Smith performed his highly visible and demanding duties with inspirational leadership, superior foresight, and resolute dedication. His amazing foresight brought great cooperation and renewed vigor to manning the fleet and promoting career opportunities. He skillfully streamlined the assignment process for over 1,800 aviation commanders and personally detailed over 1,100 helicopter aviators to critical shore and underway billets. At a time of austere manning challenges, his direct and innovative actions ensured the fleet was manned to meet the requirements of Operation ENDURING FREEDOM and the GWOT. Additionally, his analysis and recommendation of critical issues posed to the directorate were crucial to providing focus and continuity to the dynamic changes facing naval aviation.[223]

Commander, Helicopter Sea Combat Wing, U.S. Atlantic Fleet

Captain Smith led the Navy's largest aviation helicopter type wing, which included more than 5000 sailors, over one hundred aircraft, two fleet replacement squadrons, two fleet readiness centers, and a helicopter combat wing. His units performed flawlessly in Iraq and Afghanistan, providing direct combat support to Navy SEALs, direct action units, medical evacuation missions, and combat logistics.

An extremely talented operational leader, Smith expertly served as the composite helicopter air wing commander of all naval rotary-wing aircraft operations in support of Joint Task Force Katrina. Under his leadership, his team conducted intensive embarked and shore-based helicopter flight operations, including 750 sorties and 2,500 lifesaving rescue and medical evacuations.[224]

Commanding Officer, Helicopter Antisubmarine Squadron 10

Captain Smith's keen understanding of the Naval Aviator Production Process Improvement Program, combined with the streamlining of the Fleet Replacement Pilot and Fleet Replacement Aircrew programs, contributed to the graduation of 127 fleet replacement pilots and 130 fleet replacement air crewmen, which resulted in the squadron receiving the 2003 Commander Theodore G. Ellyson Aviator Production Excellence Award. Smith's innovative leadership of the maintenance effort resulted in the command's selection for the 2004 Commander, Helicopter Anti-Submarine Wing, U.S. Pacific Fleet Sikorsky Aircraft Maintenance Excellence Award. Additionally, the safety climate he fostered led the squadron to surpass over 60,000 class-A mishap-free flight hours, which resulted in the command being awarded the 2003 CNO Aviation Safety Award.[225]

Chief of Staff for Commander, Navy Cyber Forces

Captain Smith's inspirational leadership was instrumental in improving the Navy's warfighting posture in the areas of information dominance, network operations, C2, and intelligence readiness. Recognized by several external organizations for his operational savvy and keen professional judgment, Captain Smith by his direct efforts helped establish the staff and twenty-seven subordinate commands as leaders in the cyber domain, providing war-fighting capabilities to fleet and combatant commanders. He displayed exceptional resourcefulness during a period of unprecedented command change and reorganization. He significantly contributed to the successful establishment of Navy Cyber Force, U.S. Fleet Cyber Command, and the Naval Network Warfare Command.[226]

Rear Admiral Jesse A. Wilson Jr.

Background

Jesse Wilson is a native of California, Maryland. The son of a USN master chief petty officer and an elementary school teacher, he has been around the Navy his entire life.

However, he never considered joining the Navy until his junior year in Great Mills High School, when he flipped through a copy of the USNA catalog that was sitting on the coffee table in his guidance counselor's office. He went on to become one of six members of his high school class of 1982 to attend and graduate from the Naval Academy; three rose to flag rank.

He graduated from the academy with a bachelor of science in mathematics in 1986 and was commissioned an ensign in the U.S. Navy.

Significant, Operational, Policy, and Technical Contributions

Joint Warfighting Analyst on the Joint Staff

In the months after 9/11/01, Lieutenant Commander Wilson prepared and provided critical operational briefings and support to senior leaders on the Joint Staff and in the Office of the Secretary of Defense. His efforts contributed to the success of Operations ENDURING FREEDOM and NOBLE EAGLE.[227]

Commanding Officer, USS Higgins *(DDG 76)*

Commander Wilson led *Higgins* through two training cycles, a Board of Inspection and Survey visit, and a six-month western Pacific deployment with the *Nimitz* strike group. He led ASW efforts for the group, overseeing tactics alignment and improvement.[228]

Deputy Executive Assistant to the Chief of Naval Operations

Captain Wilson served as the deputy executive assistant to the twenty-eighth and twenty-ninth CNOs, Admirals Mullen and Roughead. He initiated and led a weekly forum of key staff members to prioritize and synchronize efforts across OPNAV. He adroitly advised the CNO during a dynamic period of war and strategic change.[229]

Commander, Destroyer Squadron 23 and Sea Combat Commander for the Nimitz *Strike Group*

Captain Wilson served as commodore of DESRON 23, leading the seven-ship squadron during the *Nimitz* group's 2009–10 western Pacific deployment. He instituted warfare syndicates to promulgate and develop innovative warfighting tactics.

Later, he led 1,464 personnel from all five U.S. armed services, eleven partner nations, five nongovernmental organizations, and the U.S. State Department through Pacific Partnership 2011. His strategic vision supported the Defense Forward Initiative, resulting in enhanced interoperability and increased capacity in the Pacific area of operations.[230]

Executive Assistant to the Chief of Naval Operations

Captain Wilson served as the executive assistant to the thirtieth CNO, Admiral Greenert. He oversaw the daily operations of the CNO's staff, served as personal confidant, and ensured alignment and communications across the entire OPNAV staff. He was the first African American to serve as executive assistant to the CNO.

Director, Joint Integrated Air and Missile Defense Organization

Admiral Wilson coordinated a talented team to integrate offensive and defensive cyber effects into the integrated air- and missile-defense enterprise, forging alliances with U.S. Cyber Command, U.S. Strategic Command, and the Intelligence Community to form a crosscutting implementation task force. His oversight of homeland-defense technology development-and-design planning, combined with thorough simulation in exercises NIMBLE FIRE and BLACK DART, provided lower-cost solutions to address critical defensive gaps.[231]

Commander, Carrier Strike Group 10

Admiral Wilson was directly and positively responsible for the successful employment of Carrier Strike Group 10, the USS *Dwight D. Eisenhower* carrier strike group. He displayed visionary leadership and operational brilliance in directing U.S. naval forces in Fifth and Sixth Fleet areas of responsibility during a combat deployment encompassing Operations ODYSSEY RESOLVE, OAKEN STEEL, and INHERENT RESOLVE. He led exercises with allies and regional partners, enacting a comprehensive theater security cooperation effort.

His strike group was the first to deploy in accordance with the Optimized Fleet Response Plan, requiring satisfaction of the most complex deployment certification.[232]

Director, Assessment Division, Staff of the Deputy CNO for Integration of Capabilities and Resources

Admiral Wilson was the Navy's lead for the 2016 force structure assessment that determined what the Navy's long-term force structure should be and provided the foundation for the Navy's long-range plan for construction of naval vessels. He led a team of stakeholders from across the Navy to deliver three future fleet architecture studies to Congress. Admiral Wilson then designed follow-on analysis to further refine these fleet designs, which will fundamentally change Navy procurement priorities and ensure a more dynamic and capability-focused naval force.[233]

Commander, Naval Surface Force Atlantic

In his current position, Admiral Wilson exercises administrative control of seventy ships plus fleet-support units, totaling more than 102 commands and approximately thirty-five thousand personnel stationed stateside and forward deployed in Rota, Spain, Manama, Bahrain, and Aegis Ashore Romania. He is responsible for manning, training, and equipping these forces.

Rear Admiral James W. Crawford III

Background

James W. Crawford III grew up in Charlotte, North Carolina. His mother was a teacher, his father a custodian and coach. His parents were his most significant role models. He learned about hard work at an early age, accompanying his father and paternal grand-father as they worked in the janitorial business. During summers, he worked on his maternal grandparents' tobacco farm in Clinton, North Carolina. The sweat labor he experienced during his adolescence humbled him and gave him an appreciation for the sacrifices his parents had made that paved the way for his success. Through basketball, his father taught him the importance of teamwork and the art of leadership. It was his parents' and grandparents' dedication to the smallest detail that most inspired James.

The Crawford ethos was faith, family, and education. James was the beneficiary of both the Catholic and Methodist religions. Catholic nuns, both the African American nuns of the Oblate Sisters of Providence and the Sisters of Mercy, instilled in him the importance of self-discipline, personal dignity, and respect for others. The Methodist congregation demonstrated the significance of community.

As a child of the civil rights era, James recognized that the African American strug-gle was the road to "the dream." He decided at an early age to pursue a career in the law; he viewed the law as "the great equalizer." After graduating from high school in 1975, Crawford attended Belmont Abbey College, where he played basketball, then entered the University of North Carolina School of Law. While there he was accepted into the Navy

JAG Corps student program. He elected to join the Navy because his parents gave him an understanding of sacrifice and a "commitment to something much larger than yourself." He wanted to apply the skills and knowledge acquired in law school on a big stage, in service to the nation, as the best way to repay the investment in him by his family, teachers, mentors, clerics, and others too many to mention.

As a junior officer in the JAG Corps there was no one who looked like Crawford at the level to which he aspired. But he was blessed to receive, from some very significant naval officers, opportunities that led him to where he is today. He has reflected on and tried to follow as a template what his father had told him many years ago: "Always bring your best game to the fight every day." As legendary UCLA men's basketball coach John Wooden said, it is not necessary to be the best, but rather to "be at your best when your best is needed," and to have faith that you will be given what you need to do your best.

Crawford's philosophy about life and the Navy is simple: trust in your faith; visualize your future; devise the pathway; know that obstacles are merely illusions; and be "the pebble in the pond" whose ripples wash over others so they might follow.[234]

Significant Operational, Policy, and Technical Contributions

Head, JAG Corps, Assignment and Placement Branch, Navy Personnel Command

During a period of unprecedented reorganization Navy-wide, Commander Crawford's superb performance notably enhanced the professional development and satisfied the personal desires of his constituents, while fully supporting the fleet mission. He masterfully created and monitored a two-million-dollar annual personnel transfer budget, while resourcefully adapting to budget limitations and fluctuations in funds that impacted a community of over 800 constituents. His thorough knowledge of and personal concern for his constituents made him singularly adept at detailing office personnel to assignments that proved beneficial to each officer and the Navy. This talent was confirmed when two JAG captains he nominated were selected to fill Atlantic and Pacific command staff judge advocate positions. His innovative leadership enabled his division to meet all fleet detailing needs during a period of significant organizational adjustments, downsizing, and budget constraints.[235]

Commanding Officer, Region Legal Service Office

Captain Crawford consistently displayed exceptional vision, integrity, loyalty, and tireless commitment to excellence as he successfully prosecuted more than 200 general and special courts-martial, including a number of aggravated felony cases. He masterfully transitioned the command to the RLSO structure, while providing uninterrupted support to the fleet. While leading the geographically dispersed twenty-one-office command, Captain Crawford provided superb mentoring to dozens of junior judge advocates and legal men in their professional development and commitment to service.[236]

Legal Counsel to the CJCS

Rear Admiral Crawford provided advice and counsel relating to a wide array of legal issues that were indispensable to the Chairman's ability to support the combatant commands and advise the president, the national security advisor, and the Secretary of Defense. Crawford's tremendous efforts and superb advice were key factors in the success of military operations in countering terrorism, piracy, and proliferation, as well as ongoing operations in Iraq, Afghanistan, and Libya. With equally superior effect, Rear Admiral Crawford advised the joint staff and combatant commands in HADR responses to disasters in Haiti and Japan, as well as the unique issues raised by the Arab Spring. Rear Admiral Crawford's sound judgment, professionalism, candid advice, leadership, and vision produced lasting benefits for the national security interest of the nation.[237]

Commander, Rule-of-Law Field Forces—Afghanistan, Combined Joint Interagency Task Force 435

Admiral Crawford's extraordinary vision and determination promoted the development of the rule of law and prompted Afghanistan's supreme court to improve its judicial capacity through the deployment of fifty-four Afghan judges into previously unstaffed districts. Partnered with the Afghanistan Ministry of the Interior, he developed a forensic program that built Afghanistan an evidence-based methodology as it transitioned to an advisory judicial system. Through his effective coordination efforts, he played a pivotal role in increasing the confidence of the Afghan people in their government, while simultaneously tackling insecurity in the justice sector, enhancing stability, addressing corruption, and promoting accountability at all levels of government.[238]

Rear Admiral Annie B. Andrews

Background

Annie Andrews was born in the small town of Midway, Georgia. She was one of two siblings and was reared in a strong, matriarchal, single-family home environment. She experienced her own "chain of command," as her family assigned regimented chores and services for all from an early age. Her great-grandmother lived to be 105 years old and was able to attend Annie's commissioning ceremony. Even though Annie's town was segregated, her grandmother's ownership of a country store caused Annie to mingle with a variety of individuals. Working in the store involved interacting with people of various races, which gave Annie a strong sense of service to and collaboration with others. She eventually attended Savannah State College, and in her junior year was inspired to serve in the Navy by observing and admiring the focus of the students enrolled in NROTC.

When Andrews was an ensign in 1989, there were few African American officers in the Navy, so she was often mistaken for a CPO. Some service members crossed to the other side of the street to avoid rendering her a salute. She recalled that while attending a Navy ball, some attendees mistook her for a server rather than a fellow attendee.

As a lieutenant commander, Andrews experienced problems with obtaining sufficient housing owing to her ethnicity. After obtaining orders to become the officer in charge of the Boston military entrance processing station, she phoned a realtor to inquire about housing in the area. She introduced herself and asked the realtor to identify reputable areas to live in. He responded, "I've found a great place for you. It's in an all-white neighborhood with darkies on the other side." He also stated, "You sound like a very nice person on the phone and I can't wait to meet you." The realtor mistakenly thought Andrews was Caucasian. Lieutenant Commander Andrews replied, "Great, I look forward to meeting you as well." This would be a meeting the realtor would never forget.

Andrews arrived in Boston and met the realtor. The realtor became extremely nervous, admitting that he had been expecting a "white Irish Catholic instead of a black woman." He also stated that the previously mentioned residence was now unavailable, so maybe she should consider the "opposite side of the railroad tracks for residence." Andrews demanded fair treatment from this realtor and, as her matriarchal family had taught her, she "killed him with kindness." He ultimately apologized for mistreating her on the basis of her ethnicity.

Admiral Andrews believes that for every person who meant to cause her harm in her career, there were three or four available to assist her. Her leadership philosophy is geared around the five L's: *live*—do well by others daily; *love*—always unconditionally; *learn*—continue to grow and be productive in any area; *laugh*—a hearty laugh is good for the soul; and *legacy*—be a bridge builder for others.[239]

Significant Operational, Policy, and Technical Contributions

Commander, Boston Military Entrance Processing Station

Through dynamic leadership, steadfast mission commitment, astute resource management, and unwavering concern for the welfare of her personnel, Lieutenant Commander Andrews transformed her jointly staffed command into a highly motivated and exceptionally competent team. From a tristate area encompassing Massachusetts, New Hampshire, and Rhode Island, her innovative leadership accomplished the qualification of 15,000 applicants, which greatly supported the DoD accession mission. A proactive and responsive leader, she led her team to process over 25,000 applicants without incident during her tenure. Lieutenant Commander Andrews developed an extensive crosstraining program to ensure continued efficiency, which resulted in increased flexibility in personnel assignments during personnel shortages.[240]

Head, Deserter Branch and Deserter Apprehension Program, Bureau of Naval Personnel

Lieutenant Commander Andrews displayed exceptional personnel management, unmatched resourcefulness, personal involvement, initiative, and dedication while managing the Navy's desertion and apprehension programs and policy. She managed countless time-sensitive deserter and apprehension dilemmas with federal, state, and local law enforcement officers throughout the United States. She displayed extreme tact and diplomacy, which fostered improved working relationships between military and civilian agencies. She also expertly led her team to pass a Federal Bureau of Investigation audit and process over 5000 deserters into the National Crime Information Computer system. Her efforts led directly to the Navy's location, apprehension, and safe return of 2,200 deserters to military control, which reduced the Navy's unauthorized absentee and deserter population to an all-time low. Her innovative leadership led to the consolidation of Navy absentee collection units, which reduced the Navy's manning requirements by 90 percent and saved five million dollars annually in Navy military personnel costs.[241]

Chief, Requirements Branch and Joint Manpower Planner, Directorate for Manpower and Personnel

Commander Andrews demonstrated exceptional personal drive, superior professionalism, and innovative leadership in mastering the intricacies of numerous complex joint manpower requirements. She brilliantly oversaw the daily maintenance of over 16,000 personnel requirements in the joint community and worked in concert with the Office of the Secretary of Defense in analyzing 250 budget program documents that identified and addressed unified commands' force-protection resourcing issues. She co-led the implementation of the CJCS' Joint Manpower Resource Offset plan, the first-ever mechanism for aligning joint manpower requirements on the basis of prioritized mission needs within the joint community. Her superb leadership ensured a thorough review of 12,000 CINC manpower billets in a phenomenal six-month period and the meticulous execution of a million-dollar contract. Because of her direct leadership, combatant commanders gained a first-ever link between specific mission responsibilities and the defense planning and programming capability. As the principal joint staff advocate for manpower requirements at nine unified commands, her advocacy was vital to service changes to meet global and emerging warfighter requirements.[242]

Commanding Officer, Navy Recruiting District San Francisco

Commander Andrews' personal drive and vision led the enlisted recruiting team to exceed new-contract admissions for an unprecedented fifty consecutive months, attained an accession goal unmatched for almost a decade, and earned a phenomenal third straight recruiting excellence "R" award. Her proactive leadership and clear guidance also led the officer production team to earn a third "R" award and its first-ever top-ten national ranking. She expertly guided the district into quality markets and ensured attainment of all critical mission categories and diversity goals, which significantly contributed to future fleet readiness. In addition to exceeding mission requirements, she made the personal and professional development of district sailors a top priority, which resulted in improved retention and an advancement rate above the national average.[243]

Rear Admiral Fernandez Ponds

Background

Fernandez Ponds grew up in the small community of Autaugaville, Alabama. It was located in an area, and he grew up during an era, that were "challenged" by institutional segregation and "charred" by individual racism. In effect, his hometown itself served as a catalyst for change.

Fernandez was raised by his mother and two grandparents. It was a modest upbringing of hard but honest work on a 140-acre family farm. Life was simple on the farm, but "simple" did not equate to "easy." There were challenging times, but most often he squared his shoulders and met those challenges head on.

Ponds grew up in a caring and nurturing environment, amid an extended family: a strong-willed grandfather, a nurturing grandmother, and a principled mother. He came from a long line of dreamers and doers, trailblazers and pioneers. Although the message he received was delivered in different ways, it was always the same and always clear: hard work and education will create opportunities and options for a better, brighter future.

Fernandez's mother Myrtle was the first in the family to attend college and graduate with a degree. He noted, "Mom was an African American pioneer in the field of nursing, as one of the first registered nurses to work in a primarily segregated and white-dominated medical field in Selma, Alabama. She went on to earn her degree as one of the few nurse practitioners in the area. She taught us the value of education and how difficult life could be without it."

His grandmother, known as Madia, was the youngest of sixteen children. "Madia possessed the voice of an angel and was always in demand as a soloist around the community for church events, especially funerals and home-goings. When Madia sang, it was as if God himself was speaking through her. Every song was emotionally and spiritually charged . . . ; she had 'the gift,' and it was a wondrous gift from heaven above." Leading by example, his grandmother returned to school at age fifty-five to earn her high school diploma.

His grandfather, Charlie Caver, was the patriarch of the family. "Big Daddy," as he was referred to, was the only father figure in young Fernandez Ponds' life (he never met his biological father). A sharecropper with only a third-grade education, Big Daddy was self-educated through the school of hard knocks. He found unique and industrious ways to make a living to care for his family, including his grandchildren. He taught Ponds a lot about people: how to discern words from actions, how to consider conditions and circumstance, and how to make the best of what you had. He was a man's man, and everyone in the community respected him for his wit and his will. Although he stood only about 5'9", he was a giant of a man, and a man without fear.

When asked about his hometown of Autaugaville, Admiral Ponds described his childhood as being reared at the crossroads of the civil rights movement, with Birmingham to the north, Montgomery to the east, and Selma to the west. Growing up, Ponds was inspired, as Dr. Martin Luther King Jr. championed civil rights in his home state, including very near his hometown. Although Ponds' family and others in the community tried their best to shield and protect Fernandez and his siblings from the "unpleasantness" of segregation and racism, vivid memories of the images and vestiges of hate, anger, and contempt for those of color remained seared into his mind.

However, Ponds also benefited from those who helped create opportunities. Some call them mentors, but he refers to them as "life coaches." His school vice principal was a retired African American Marine who neither took any lip nor accepted any excuses from anyone who did not try their very best to be their very best. He was not self-righteous, but he was always right in Ponds' mind. During a time when corporal punishment was not a criminal act, the vice principal often introduced those who behaved badly to a paddle that hung on the wall openly behind his desk. That paddle was a constant reminder that "uncomfortable" consequences followed "unacceptable" behavior.

Another standout was Fernandez's English teacher. A well-dressed, rather young African American female graduate from a nearby HBCU, she pulled no punches and had "zero tolerance" for the use of improper English. She always reminded him that the spoken word, when used properly, was a force to be reckoned with. She did not belittle those who used improper grammar, but emphasized that if one wanted to be recognized and respected in this world, he or she would need to command the English language, "the price of admission to the exciting world of education." This type of teaching was nothing new to Fernandez, as his folks felt the same way and did not tolerate the use of words such as *ain't, cain't,* and other improper derivatives of the English language. Ponds recalled "a number of raps on the beak for spouting unrecognizable or unacceptable phrases."

His band teacher was also a prominent figure early in Ponds' life. This teacher could play every instrument and had the unique ability to make every student feel special and gifted. He was a good man, and many students confided their problems to him. The teacher did not consider himself a fixer, but he was a great listener, and most often that was all his students needed: an ear, not an earful.

Fernandez's favorite teacher in the entire school system was an African American male science instructor. The young man considered this instructor simply brilliant. He taught physics, biology, chemistry—all the tough classes that students dreaded. Through science, he opened up a whole new world—to those who dared to take, and stay in, his classes. Fernandez did so. This teacher was disciplined, methodical, and very demanding; but he was also dedicated and fiercely loyal. Fernandez recalls him saying that "if you apply the right process and procedure, you'll get the right answer," and those words stuck with him, such that he remains a disciple of that approach to this day.

However, as counterpoint to all the possibilities to which these mentors opened him during his seminal years, there remained a very prominent barrier: the high school principal. One school day, Fernandez and three other fifth-grade African American males were summoned to the principal's office. None of them knew why they had been summoned; they were wide-eyed and slightly panicked. He remembers walking into the office and seeing larger-than-life-sized portraits of the man positioned beside those of President George Washington.

The principal wasted no time explaining the trouble toward which they were headed. As the boys remained standing, he leaned across his large, antique desk and stated, "I hear you have been playing with the white girls. I just want you to know, that type of behavior will not be tolerated, and if you continue you will be expelled." He went on to explain that the authorities had "brought over" enough "little black girls" to play with, so there was no reason for them to play with white girls.

The boys left the office scared, humiliated, and deflated. It was terrible blow. Two of them went on to succeed and graduate, but the others never recovered and did not receive their high school diplomas. Ponds is not certain whether that single event was the cause of the latter, but he believes that seeds of hopelessness and despair that were planted on that day would prove decisive, if not devastating, in those boys' lives by creating a vicious cycle of lowered expectations.

But Ponds did graduate from high school, and subsequently the University of Alabama. Then he decided to join the Navy via OCS. Of his three siblings, two have served in the U.S. Navy: his older brother served as a radioman, and his younger brother became CO of an *Arleigh Burke*-class guided-missile destroyer. Fernandez is very proud of them both, his older brother for breaking with a family tradition of serving in the U.S. Army and his younger brother for blazing his own trail as a successful naval officer. In his own case, he considers his decision to be an act of boldness: he was choosing his own destiny instead of accepting the lowered expectations others set while he grew up in "the heart of Dixie."

Ponds faced initial challenges during his early Navy years, such as learning maritime vernacular, seamanship, and navigation—and how to swim. He recalls that during OCS he spent numerous early-morning and late-evening hours at the pool so he could pass the third-class swim test. Academically, he often studied after taps, with a flashlight. He leaned on classmates to learn maneuvering board concepts and to master the art and science of piloting and celestial navigation. He gives a lot of credit to the OCS officers and senior enlisted personnel and his company classmates for their support and teamwork.

Upon commissioning, Ponds' first ship tour was as damage control assistant on an ammunition auxiliary ship. It was very challenging; he believes this to be the toughest job for a first-tour ensign. Reporting directly to the CO and XO for the safety and training of the entire ship in damage control was very intimidating. It was even tougher being DCA while trying to earn his surface warfare officer pin. However, there was a big benefit to being responsible for the entire ship: having to know the entire ship—bow to stern, port to starboard, and mast to keel.

Ponds was fortunate to have a very patient CO, a sharp XO, and an insightful department head to help him get through it, not to mention four very close fellow ensigns, all of whom reported on board within weeks of one another, only months prior to a six-month deployment—a true green team! During this assignment, Ponds quickly learned how to assimilate, cooperate, and communicate to get the crew's support. The chiefs' mess was his favorite place. He quickly learned the value of the CPO and embraced the concept of "Go ask the chief." The members of the chiefs' mess—the "goat locker"—taught and taunted simultaneously, and Ponds was grateful for both. Eventually they accepted him as an honorary CPO.

Ponds believes that his upbringing in the South enabled him to adapt to change and to shrug off, if not wave off, covert and sometimes overt acts of bias, while embracing acts of kindness. He also believes that the lessons he learned during his first shipboard tour carried him through subsequent tours of duty throughout his Navy career. Through it all, he understands that he was the beneficiary of those who believed in him and would not allow him to give up or fail. His family; shipmates, peers, and colleagues; subordinates; and commanders and supervisors played prominent roles in his career and life—they were "the inspiration to my many aspirations." Ponds feels that he arrived at flag officer status standing in the footprints and on the shoulders of giants such as Admirals Gravely, Fishburne, Reason, and others.[244]

Significant, Operational, Policy, and Technical Contributions

Inspections Division, Naval Inspector General

Commander Ponds' comprehensive issue papers on manpower, training, material, IT, and logistics during six command inspections and several area visits significantly contributed to improving fleet readiness and the quality of life for sailors, Marines, and DoD civilians and their families worldwide. He developed and implemented a database management system for automating, tracking, and coordinating follow-up actions on over 4,300 formal inspection recommendations. He was a pivotal member of the IT infrastructure team during Year 2000 assessments and he was instrumental to other vital studies of future ship design and shore infrastructure requirements for the twenty-first-century Navy.[245]

Mission Commander and Task Group Commander, HADR Operations in Haiti

Commodore Ponds was a strong and visionary force and displayed charismatic leadership, tireless effort, and unmatched commitment. As commander of Task Group 40.4, he conducted rapid-response crisis-action planning while steaming USS *Kearsarge* over 400 miles to arrive off the coast of Port-au-Prince within thirty-six hours of Haiti's natural disaster. Within forty-eight hours he began to execute flawlessly a sixteen-day international and interagency HADR mission with partner nations, the UN, and several other organizations. His efforts directly contributed to the minimization of loss of life and mitigation of human suffering for the people of Haiti. As mission commander for Operation CONTINUING PROMISE-08, he creatively executed a complex four-month humanitarian and civic assistance mission to five Latin America and Caribbean nations that involved U.S. joint armed services, U.S. government agencies, nongovernmental organizations, and partner nations.

Ponds' team triaged over 47,000 patients, conducted 199,550 medical treatment encounters, completed 24 engineering projects, completed 51 subject matter expert exchanges, and dispensed 199 pallets of civic action Project Handclasp materials. Commodore Ponds singularly and effectively advanced U.S. policies, U.S. maritime strategy, and USSOUTHCOM's theater security cooperation and HADR initiatives. His efforts effectively expanded an array of military-to-military and nation-to-nation programs that improved interoperability and accelerated the modernization of regional navies, while significantly enhancing stability and security for this region.[246]

Branch Head, Air-Sea Battle Office

Captain Ponds effectively and efficiently led the Navy's implementation efforts for the air-sea battle concept. He worked extensively with counterparts in the Air Force and Marine Corps in establishing the Tri-Service Air-Sea Battle Office and wrote the memorandum of understanding that aligned the three services and developed the governance structure for the office. He played a vital role in creating and developing a strategic communications plan for the Air-Sea Battle Office that educated and influenced a broad spectrum of stakeholders.

While working in close cooperation with analysts and planners from USPACOM and USCENTCOM, Ponds developed a comprehensive, prioritized list of material solutions to the nation's most serious anti-access/area-denial challenges and integrated them into the Planning, Programming, Budgeting, and Execution Process to meet future strategic objectives.[247]

Rear Admiral Dwight D. Shepherd

Background

Dwight Shepherd's roots extend from the small town of Burnt Corn, Alabama, but he was reared in Cleveland, Ohio, because his family moved there for better employment opportunities. He is from a two-family home, and his father and grandfather were both steel mill workers. His grandfather was an early inspiration; his favorite expression was "If you love the work you do, then you never have to work a day in your life." Dwight's father was his baseball coach starting from Little League at age seven and extending through his high school years. Dwight's entire family was very familiar with hard work and demanded that he be respectful of others.

After graduating from high school, Dwight attended the University of Cincinnati. Although his father and grandfather had served in the Army, they did not encourage him to join the military. However, during a minority recruiting fair at the university, he saw a picture of a Tomcat aircraft on display, and was asked if he would like to fly it. He spoke briefly with the recruiter, but still was not interested in the military. A few months later, he received offers from the business community but was unable to secure his dream job, which was to work for Procter and Gamble. He reencountered—under a pile of mail—a Navy pamphlet in which he read about pilots earning 20,000 dollars while in flight school. That was comparable to the pay at Procter and Gamble, so he called the recruiter, who convinced him to join the Navy. He was also inspired to join the Navy by viewing the video "Pressure Point" and the movie "An Officer and a Gentleman."

After being accepted into flight school, Shepherd was introduced to aerodynamics and other engineering-related disciplines. AOCS was also very challenging because it represented the first time he had to assimilate into an environment different from his surroundings in Cleveland. He understood early that because he looked different from most of his colleagues, moments of "notoriety" would occur frequently. He recalled his grandfather's advice: "You have to make a great first impression; and since you're different, you'll be noticed, so use it to your advantage." He never forgot his grandfather's wise words, and they were a significant reason he attained flag status in the Navy.[248]

Significant Operational, Policy, and Technical Contributions

Commanding Officer, Fleet Air Reconnaissance Squadron 3

Commander Shepherd's inspirational leadership, with an emphasis on mission readiness, enabled his squadron to execute 1,388 sorties, 60,000 mishap-free flight hours, and the flawless expenditure of a 12.5-million-dollar budget. During USSTRATCOM's GLOBAL GUARDIAN exercise in 2002, his visionary planning produced the squadron's first generation of eight aircrews and deployment of seven E-6B aircraft that yielded an unprecedented 100 percent continuous airborne coverage. Commander Shepherd's squadron attained a remarkable level of operational excellence and achieved a mission-capable rate that exceeded the CNO's goal by 4 percent. His proactive leadership was instrumental in the squadron having zero discrepancies during the 2002 NATO operations evaluation.[249]

Assistant Chief of Staff for C4I and Information Warfare Commander, Carrier Strike Group 5

Commander Shepherd displayed innovative leadership and was the driving force behind C4I support to Carrier Strike Group 5 during ten major exercises. He provided tremendous operational insight during the ongoing development of contingency planning for U.S.-Japanese bilateral theater missile-defense multilink and common operational picture architecture development. He contributed significantly to the coordination of C4I installations in and modifications to one aircraft carrier, three guided-missile cruisers, two frigates, and a host of destroyers. As the information warfare commander, he improved the readiness of forward-deployed naval forces by expertly integrating information-warfare tactics, techniques, and procedures into fighting directives and response plans of both the air-defense commander and the sea-combat commander.[250]

Commander, Strategic Communication Wing 1 and Commander, Task Force 124

Captain Shepherd's visionary outlook in operations and training, in addition to his financial insights, laid the foundation for future advances in naval aviation for years to come. He pioneered new operational tactics, mission plans, and new initiatives in joint operations.

Shepherd also built the framework for multiple major aircraft modification programs for the E-6B Mercury airframe, as well as spearheading the first-ever forward deployment of the E-6B aircraft, which provided critical C3 in the USCENTCOM area of responsibility. This resulted in direct support of Operation IRAQI FREEDOM and helped lead to successful mission accomplishment.

Captain Shepherd also made significant contributions to the diversity of the force, becoming a charter member of the Senior Diversity Council, which shapes and develops diversity in naval aviation.[251]

Rear Admiral Willie L. Metts

Background

Willie Metts was raised in the small town of Danville, Georgia. His father died when he was three years old, leaving his mother to raise five children alone. His mother succeeded in instilling the value of hard work, dedication, and a positive attitude in all her children from an early age. As a youngster, Willie always went out of his way to help people, and his mother was always proud of him for behaving in that manner. His family was poor in terms of financial prosperity but rich in moral character, and he did not feel poor because all their needs were met.

While attending high school, Willie's intellectual aspirations to reach beyond his hometown led his band director to take him along during college trips; the young Metts was friends with the band director's son, so he gained the opportunity to travel with the family. This "set the hook" for Metts to view college as a real possibility. Initially, he wanted to become a member of Congress; however, he decided to serve his country in another capacity by joining the military.

After graduating from high school, a lack of financial assistance led Willie to pursue admission to Savannah State College, and in the spring of his freshman year to enroll in the NROTC scholarship program.

Metts started his Navy career as a surface warfare officer, but after assessing his career goals he decided to pursue a lateral transfer into the cryptology community. Transferring laterally into another community is never an easy task, but he worked as hard as he could and maintained a positive attitude.

Metts also adhered to the moral principles his mother had taught him. These principles afforded him the opportunity to excel in his chosen Navy community. He had wonderful mentors who exposed him to various naval operations, and he credits their mentorship and servant leadership for providing the opportunities that made it possible for him to achieve flag rank.[252]

Significant, Operational, Policy, and Technical Contributions

Director, Commander's Initiatives Group and Special Assistant for Commander, Pacific Fleet

Commander Metts displayed exceptional leadership and keen foresight in articulating and promoting U.S. Pacific Fleet priorities and strategies. An exceptional communicator, he brilliantly advanced a clear understanding of the commander's goals and the strategy to effect change positively throughout the Pacific. As the U.S. Pacific Fleet commander's single voice and principal liaison with Congress and DoD staffs, he profoundly influenced key issues shaping Navy positions in the Pacific for years to come. Additionally, he demonstrated superb operational acumen in developing and implementing the first Pacific Fleet and Joint Task Force 519 effects-based operational campaign and a commander's focus area assessment process that markedly influenced every aspect of naval force employment through the Asia-Pacific region.[253]

Commanding Officer, Navy Information Operations Command Hawaii

Captain Metts' innovative leadership and uncommon vision drove information warfare community improvements that culminated in the establishment of the fleet information operations center, which met the increased demand signal from combatant and maritime commanders for information-operation capabilities. As a result of his significant leadership and unwavering focus, the command facilitated the integration of sailors into the NSA and Hawaii's computer network operations divisions, which enabled the first-ever national support to real-time active computer networks for units deployed in the western Pacific.

Metts' leadership precipitated 100 percent achievement of the command's individual augmentation requirements, while simultaneously meeting the largest fleet direct support requirements in the history of the command.[254]

Deputy Chief, Tailored Access Operations, Signals Intelligence Directorate, National Security Agency

Admiral Metts' outstanding leadership and ceaseless efforts resulted in major contributions to the national security of the United States. He led thousands of civilian and military personnel with highly technical capabilities and oversaw a budget exceeding half a billion dollars. His direct efforts enabled high-priority cyber support to combatant commanders and civil agencies worldwide. His innovative thinking and personal commitment in planning and conducting computer network exploitation established him as a driving force behind DoD and NSA policy. He was instrumental in developing critical agreements and concepts of operation to meet the rapid growth of cyber operations as part of traditional military operations, and he expanded intelligence support, which met the needs of both national intelligence and combatant command operations. Admiral Metts was directly responsible for developing and implementing the plan that enhanced support to cyber defense for critical U.S. infrastructure and formed the foundation of the U.S. Cyber Command's Cyber Mission Force.[255]

Rear Admiral Eric C. Young

Background

Eric Young grew up in the small town of Abilene, Texas. His mother, a housekeeper, was the family's primary provider. One of four siblings, Eric credits his success to his mother and to his older brother, now a police officer, who served as a mentor and inspiration for what would later be an influential career.

Young attributes his work ethic and core values to his mother. Education was a priority she instilled in him from an early age. Having previously completed a tenth-grade education, she went back to school when Eric was ten years old, received her GED, then entered the medical field as a practicing nurse. She believed in hard work and earning what she received; there was no expectation of a handout in Young's family. All the children were taught that if they wanted something, they would have to work hard to earn it.

Young's mother also demonstrated the importance of always maintaining a positive attitude, regardless of circumstance. Her nickname in her community was "the singing nurse" for her ability to carry a gospel tune during the most challenging situations. Well after his mother's unfortunate passing, Young would continue to mirror her optimistic approach to life, including throughout his Navy career both at sea and ashore.

Eric was a youth during the era of the civil rights movement; for instance, he was the only African American in his third-grade class. During that time, he remained undeterred, remembering to stay optimistic and always try his hardest, whether the challenge was big or small. His "can-do" attitude showed in his academic achievements, and eventually he was accepted into Angelo State University in Abilene, Texas, where he majored in chemistry.

A scientist at heart, Young's natural ability for research and numbers led to a position in the civilian sector conducting research. That turned out to be only a short deviation; it did not take long in the corporate world before Young concluded he needed to expand his horizons, to seek broader opportunities outside the borders of his small hometown. The big question for him was how to do it.

There was no military presence in Abilene, and certainly there were no recruiters. But Young did have a sister-in-law in the Air Force—and he did see the movie "An Officer and a Gentlemen" in 1982. The movie showed Young the opportunities and virtues of a military career, inspiring him to join the service. Young surprised his family with a life-altering decision that would take him out of his small town in Texas—and influence future policy and the lives of over 100,000 sailors.

Young met with a recruiter, attended OCS, and received his commission as an ensign in February 1985. He reported to his first command as the ordnance officer. This was a challenging time for Ensign Young; adjusting to the Navy after growing up in Abilene was not easy. Among other things, there were speech challenges, and no one took the time to mentor him. He really wanted to get out of the Navy; if not for the leadership of his wife, he would have done so.

This changed when his CO was relieved. The new CO mentored Ensign Young, but was very frank with him. He told him, "I see a lot of potential in you, but frankly, I need you to work twice as hard because you're a minority on this ship. You'll have to work harder, and everything you get, you're gonna have to earn it." After this word from his CO, Young qualified faster and was awarded two Navy Achievement Medals. That talk transformed his Navy career, and the experience shaped his current leadership philosophy: "Leadership starts from the top, with the CO. A CO can change a life if he (or she) is in tune with his people."

During his subsequent tours as an active-duty surface warfare officer and later as a reservist, Young held true to his mother's educational ethos, achieving both a master of science degree in financial management from the Naval Postgraduate School and a master of arts degree in national security and strategic studies from the Naval War College in Newport, Rhode Island.

As the culmination of his life's work, Young completed his career as a U.S. Navy officer in 2016, having reached the highest position that a full-time support sailor can achieve: the rank of two-star admiral and a position as commander, Navy Reserve Forces Command.[256]

Significant Operational, Policy, and Technical Contributions

Weapons Control Officer, USS Reid (FFG 30)

Lieutenant (junior grade) Young displayed exceptional skill and resourcefulness as his ship provided vital assistance under the most adverse conditions during the rescue effort for USS *Stark* (FFG 31) after the latter received two missile hits on May 17, 1987. Unsure of the threat of further attack, Young's direct efforts in damage control and rendering of medical assistance was inspiring to all who observed him, and his bold courage and total dedication to duty were in keeping with the highest traditions of naval service.[257]

Manpower Analyst, Staff of Deputy CNO

Commander Young possessed superb analytical skill and competency, which made him the focal point for executing diverse and challenging surface warfare manpower issues. As the executive for the Navy's second largest manpower resource sponsor in the early 2000s, he superbly managed 2.5 billion dollars in active and reserve personnel funds. He specifically crafted a seventeen-billion-dollar manpower budget for the surface warfare community balanced across the Future Years Defense Plan.[258]

Chief Staff Officer to Commander, Amphibious Squadron 11

Captain Young was a true "amphibious warrior" and mentor, as he exercised steadfast leadership, determination, and flexibility, while changing the force's focus from war fighting to HADR to provide critical lifesaving support and temporary living quarters and distribute 50,000 dollars in relief goods to over 1,500 evacuees and mudslide victims after the devastating mudslide in Leyte, Philippines, in February 2006.

Young's strategic focus and creativity were the impetus behind COMPHIBRON 11's many successes in theater security engagements. His direct influence was crucial to the development and execution of Expeditionary Strike Group 7's plan of action, as well as the milestone implementations within COMPHIBRON 11 to support the successful certification to the *Essex* expeditionary strike group.[259]

Commander, Destroyer Squadron 1

As the immediate superior in command, Captain Young ensured his ships possessed the material readiness and war-fighting proficiency necessary to conduct forward fleet operations, including support to Operations IRAQI FREEDOM and ENDURING FREEDOM. As Carrier Strike Group 1 sea-combat commander, he directed full-spectrum operations around South America and assumed all operational responsibility for multinational surface ship operations in support of Operation UNIFIED RESPONSE earthquake relief to Haiti.

Young spearheaded the planning and coordination efforts for PEACE TRITON, a complex, multifaceted foreign military sales-related support program between the United States and Singapore. As sea-combat commander for amphibious forces during RIMPAC 2010, the world's largest multinational maritime exercise, he demonstrated exceptional operational prowess while planning and executing dozens of supporting events.[260]

Deputy Director, Training, OASD for Reserve Affairs

Captain Young's superb leadership and agile, adaptive thinking contributed to national security and the improved readiness of over 1.1 million reserve-component service members. Using his extraordinary leadership ability to learn and appreciate service cultural nuances, he developed an intricate understanding of complex training issues and led collaborative working group efforts involving key DoD personnel. His significant leadership propelled the expert facilitation of the Regional Integrated Training Environment initiative and the Ancillary Training and General Military Working Group. These initiatives successfully increased joint interdependence among reserve components and harvested efficiencies to mitigate an increasingly austere budget environment. This contributed to the preservation of the operational reserve as an indispensable component of national security, defense, and military strategies.[261]

Rear Admiral Stephen C. Evans

Background

Rear Admiral Evans, a native of Beaufort, South Carolina, is the son of a U.S. Marine. Throughout his childhood, his parents encouraged him to set high goals and not let anyone impose limitations or ceilings on what he could become or accomplish. Growing up in a military family, Stephen received as a foundation the necessity for service, a sense of duty, and the importance of reaching out to help others reach achievements beyond what they could have imagined or thought possible. These strong principles have served as his foundation throughout life.

Evans attended The Citadel in Charleston, South Carolina, earned a Bachelor of Arts in history, and graduated in 1986. All students at The Citadel are members of the Corps of Cadets and participate in the ROTC program, in which Evans earned Advanced Standing. Although Evans had not intended originally to serve in the military following college, one of his mentors saw potential for him to be an influential leader as a military officer. Although his mother always had wanted to see him sharply dressed in the Marines' service dress uniform, Evans was commissioned as an ensign in the Navy.

Evans entered the surface warfare officer community. He had planned on serving his obligated three years, then pursuing a law degree, but eventually he realized all the opportunities and adventure a career in the Navy offered.

Significant Operational, Policy, and Technical Contributions

Executive Officer, USS Hué City *(CG 66)*

Lieutenant Commander Evans' inspirational leadership and superior managerial skills were the driving force behind *Hué City's* exceptional performance.

During engineering initial assessment, underway demonstration, *John F. Kennedy* battle-group workups, and all interdeployment training-cycle milestones, his strategic vision and high standards ensured *Hué City* earned her third consecutive battle efficiency award, successfully completed five years of cooperative engagement capability testing and evaluation, and achieved an unmatched level of combat matériel and mission readiness. His direct oversight and months of planning for inspection and survey culminated in the board of Atlantic Fleet inspection and survey noting *Hué City's* inspection as one of the most prepared and flawlessly coordinated evolutions to date.

His contagious optimism and work ethic inspired *Hué City's* crew to perform at the highest of standards and his leadership has been the keystone for *Hué City's* achievement of combat-ready excellence.

Commanding Officer, USS Mitscher *(DDG 57)*

Captain Evans' superb performance of duty, extraordinary vision, and total professionalism epitomize the qualities inherent in command at sea.

Displaying consummate skill and inspiring leadership, he guided *Mitscher* through a demanding deployment to the Mediterranean Sea with NATO forces in support of Operation ACTIVE ENDEAVOR. His flawless performance as Commander, Task Group 440.01, while coordinating the movements and operations of twelve NATO warships, three submarines, and four maritime patrol aircraft, garnered praise from the NATO maritime component commander for the southern region.

His "mission first, people always" approach ensured the ship's success during a compressed interdeployment training cycle and ensured that *Mitscher* deployed 100 percent combat ready. A talented and charismatic mentor dedicated to fulfilling the potential of every sailor, he dramatically improved morale and esprit de corps aboard *Mitscher*, earning the Golden Anchor for retention excellence.

Deputy Commander, Destroyer Squadron 24

Captain Evans' exceptional leadership, vision, and outstanding judgment ensured the success of Strike Force Training Atlantic and Destroyer Squadron 24 operational-mission, fleet-training, and theater security-cooperation objectives. Throughout his fifteen-month tour, Captain Evans decisively executed his responsibilities while safely and effectively leading more than twenty-five ships in conducting over 120 days of at-sea fleet operations to achieve mission success.

Utilizing his vast operational experience and tactical prowess, he provided ready maritime surface forces for global assignment, greatly enhancing U.S. relationships with coalition partners from twenty-four nations in execution of the maritime strategy. He orchestrated the planning and execution of Second Fleet's fleet irregular warfare training, a robust, comprehensive, and repeatable exercise at sea that significantly improved commanding officer and ship readiness for intense disaggregated operations while forward deployed.

An exceptional leader by every standard, Captain Evans' tremendous work ethic, technical innovation, and selfless leadership by example made Destroyer Squadron 24 the premier and most-ready group of fighting ships in the Atlantic Fleet.

Commander, Destroyer Squadron 50

Captain Evans provided operational oversight to eleven forward-deployed Navy and Coast Guard patrol boat commanders and thirteen frigates and destroyers assigned to Task Force 55. His energetic leadership led to the development and refinement of SPARTAN KOPIS, a counter-fast attack-craft and fast inshore attack-craft exercise.

Captain Evans' vision ensured the flawless transition of Task Force 152 to a coalition staff based in Bahrain, which significantly improved interoperability with regional allies. His efforts resulted in the development of standardized maritime security exercises and focused operations to highlight illicit activity in the Arabian Gulf. In addition, he expertly planned and supervised execution of the U.S. Naval Forces Central Command's bilateral surface exercise program.

Director, Division of Professional Development, U.S. Naval Academy

Captain Evans' insightful planning, sound judgment, and inspirational leadership significantly enhanced operational and training readiness. He led a diverse staff of forty-seven officers, 200 enlisted personnel, and seventy-five civilian personnel providing safe training to over 6000 midshipmen, utilizing a combination of modern training facilities, bridge simulators, and a fleet of 211 watercraft. His dedication to enhancing midshipman training opportunities and improving the quality of life of the men and women assigned to his command produced outstanding levels of productivity and professional development.

In support of midshipman summer training, Captain Evans directed planning and execution of a $2.7 million program that achieved 7000 individual fleet cruise assignments, with an unprecedented 95 percent fleet contact for midshipmen, along with yard patrol and sail craft training that safely deployed over 3000 midshipmen worldwide. Continuing a program of world-class excellence, Captain Evans oversaw all sailing programs, which included the nationally ranked (seventh-place) dinghy team and varsity and junior varsity offshore programs. His attention to all safety and operational risk-management processes, coupled with an aggressive phased-maintenance plan, significantly improved material readiness and availability, while maintaining an unblemished safety record.

As a member of the admissions board, he was instrumental in leading a team that reviewed a total of 31,230 applications to identify the most qualified men and women for the classes of 2013 and 2014.

Senior Military Assistant to the Secretary of the Navy

Captain Evans' superior performance, personal loyalty, and unmatched professionalism were a direct and extraordinary benefit to the Secretary of the Navy and the larger Navy and Marine Corps team. Drawing from a wide range of operational and staff experiences, he provided invaluable support and expert advice across the spectrum of issues facing the Department of the Navy during a period of exceptional fiscal challenges.

He worked tirelessly across multiple organizations to ensure the Secretary's priorities of taking care of sailors and Marines, developing and cultivating a spirit of innovation, achieving acquisition excellence, and putting an end to sexual assault were well understood and effectively prioritized. Captain Evans' seasoned perspective and skilled approach when working with the Secretariat, office of the Secretary of Defense, members of Congress, the White House, and our international partners were critical to successful outcomes in countless instances. These same skills were instrumental in addressing a myriad of issues with both the Navy and Marine Corps headquarters staff. His positive, "teamwork" approach greatly enhanced the overall effectiveness of the Secretariat and ensured seamless cooperation with the highest levels of the Department of the Navy.

Commander, Naval Service Training Command

Rear Admiral Evans provided inspirational leadership and ensured excellence in all endeavors, as each initiative implemented under his guidance enhanced the safety, quality of life, and high-velocity learning of more than 100,000 recruits, officer candidates, and midshipmen.

He supported separate cross-functional teams that culminated in a major revision to the officers Professional Core Competencies manual and the inaugural recruit Basic Military Training Core Competencies manual to ensure that curriculum and standards in the Navy's accessions training programs meet the needs of the fleet.

He also delivered essential guidance toward implementation of the Alternative Naval Reserve Officers Training Corps scholarship restructure proposal, expertly drawing from numerous databases to finitely project future production costs, realizing more than twelve million dollars in annual savings by precision-loading scholarships, while still meeting or exceeding the Navy's officer-accession goals.

Rear Admiral Alvin Holsey

Background

Alvin Holsey is a native of Fort Valley, GA, and a 1983 graduate of Peach County High School. His role models were his parents, who taught him the importance of service, humility, and respect. His father served in the Army during the Korean War, and his seven uncles all served in the Navy or Army, from Korea to Vietnam and DESERT STORM.

In the fall of 1983, Alvin attended Morehouse College, with aspirations of pursuing a career in aviation. During his sophomore year, he received an NROTC scholarship and joined the recently established NROTC unit serving the historically black colleges and universities in Atlanta University Center. In 1988, he earned a degree in computer science and received his commission. Holsey is that NROTC unit's first officer to be selected for command and flag rank. In the 150-year history of Morehouse, he is the second graduate to be promoted to flag or general officer.

Following primary and advanced flight training, Holsey was designated a naval aviator in 1989 at NAS Whiting Field in Milton, FL. He later earned a Master of Science in management from Troy State University in 1995 and completed the Joint Forces Staff College in 2010.

Significant Technical, Operational, and Policy Contributions

Rear Admiral Holsey served in a variety of training and operational squadrons, including Helicopter Anti-Submarine Squadrons, Light (HSLs) 36, 37, 40, and 44 and Helicopter

Training Squadron 8. During his career, Holsey amassed over 4000 flight hours in a variety of aircraft. His sea assignments included deployments aboard USS *Jesse L. Brown* (FF 1089), USS *Nicholson* (DD 982), USS *Vreeland* (FF 1068), USS *Vella Gulf* (CG 72), USS *Gettysburg* (CG 64), USS *Simpson* (FFG 56), and USS *Makin Island* (LHD 8).

Assignments to shore and staff billets included flag aide to Commander, Naval Air Forces; Deputy Chief of Naval Operations (Warfare Requirements and Programs N6/N7); operations officer on the Joint Chiefs of Staff, J-3; Joint Operations Directorate, European Command; deputy director, PERS 43/Head Air Combat Placement Officer, Navy Personnel Command; force operations officer, N3 at Commander, Naval Air Forces, U.S. Pacific Fleet; and executive assistant to the Chief of Naval Operations.

Commanding Officer, HSL-37

In 2007, Commander Holsey assumed command of the Easy Riders of HSL-37. Under his guidance, the Easy Riders deployed seven detachments in support of twenty exercises, two carrier strike groups, and two expeditionary strike groups in support of Operations ENDURING FREEDOM and IRAQI FREEDOM. He vigorously championed new technologies and tactics in support of fleet weapons development and evaluations, while instituting one of the most rigorous tactical training programs in the Light Airborne Multi-Purpose System (LAMPS) community.

His squadron was recognized with the Captain Arnold J. Isbell Award for tactical excellence and the Navy League's 2007 Admiral Vern Clark Award for safety. His involved leadership enabled the squadron to excel in over twenty-five maintenance inspections, while his sailors earned over one hundred maintenance qualifications and achieved a remarkable 67 percent reenlistment rate.[262]

Commanding Officer, USS Makin Island (LHD 8)

Captain Holsey served as the fourth commanding officer of the amphibious assault ship *Makin Island,* the Navy's first diesel-electrical hybrid-propulsion ship. Holsey deftly guided his crew of 1,100 sailors and Marines through a compressed, blended maintenance and training phase, completing a fourteen-month phased maintenance availability, while certifying in nineteen mission-warfare areas with an impressive 95 percent overall figure of merit.

While deployed in Fifth Fleet, *Makin Island* directly supported Operations INHERENT RESOLVE and IRAQI UNITY, during which Holsey's team supported tactical recovery of aircraft and personnel and casualty-evacuation alert missions, as well as multiple reconnaissance and close-air-support missions into Iraq and Syria. During his tenure aboard, *Makin Island* earned a second Captain Edward F. Ney Memorial Food Service Award and a seventh consecutive Retention Excellence Award.[263]

Deputy Director for Operations, Joint Staff, J3

Rear Admiral Holsey currently serves as one of five deputy directors for operations in the National Joint Operations and Intelligence Center at the Pentagon. In this role, he plans and directs the actions for a Joint Staff officer/enlisted operations team performing worldwide monitoring, crisis-response actions, and strategic nuclear command-and-control (C2) watch functions. Additionally, he apprises the Chairman, Secretary of Defense, and president of potential conventional, cyber, and nuclear threats against the United States or its allies. His efforts are key to the 24/7 coordination and synchronization of routine and contingency C2 activities on behalf of the Chairman, which directly supports the unified combatant commands.[264]

THE U.S. NAVY'S CENTENNIAL SEVEN

The U. S. submarine force was established in the first decade of the 1900s. Within the first hundred years of its existence, to the year 2000, seven African Americans commanded Navy submarines. These skippers became known as the Centennial Seven. The seven (and the boats they commanded) were Captain Pete Tzomes (USS *Houston*), Rear Admiral Tony Watson (USS *Jacksonville*), Commander Will Bundy (USS *Barbel*), Vice Admiral Mel Williams Jr. (USS *Nebraska*), Captain Joe Peterson (USS *Dolphin*), Admiral Cecil Haney (USS *Honolulu*), and Vice Admiral Bruce Grooms (USS *Asheville*).

L-R: Capt. Pete Tzomes (Ret.), Rear Adm. Tony Watson (Ret.), Dr. Will Bundy, Vice Adm. Mel Williams (Ret.), Capt. Joe Peterson (Ret.), Adm. Cecil Haney, and Vice Adm. Bruce Grooms

A note on submarines: by being silently at sea every day, strategic ballistic-missile submarines play a critical role in our nation's strategic defense: deterring potential adversaries from employing weapons of mass destruction against the United States. Keeping each submarine platform at sea for a higher percentage of the time requires two separate crews (designated Blue and Gold); one crew is at sea on patrol while the other rests, then trains for the next at-sea period.

Captain C. A. 'Pete' Tzomes

Background

Pete Tzomes, the older of two children in his family, was born in Williamsport, Pennsylvania, in 1944 to James and Charlotte Tzomes. He was reared in an environment in which racism was rampant; the use of [the N-word] was commonplace; in fact, there was a street in Williamsport called "N-Hollow." In a recent interview about his background, Tzomes stated, "Kids who were ten or eleven years old would call my father by his first name, and that just used to bother me, but back in those days, that came with the turf. That was part of the way of keeping you in your place."[265]

Even though his initial surroundings were not conducive to promoting academic equality, Tzomes' mother and father taught him that having a good attitude and a strong work ethic would triumph in the end. But Tzomes' ambitions were influenced by his surroundings too: "There were three things I was thinking about doing when I grew up: a professional baseball player, a garbage man, or a pimp. . . . I had no role models. The reason that I thought about those is because I just thought that's how I could make money."[266]

Then he saw a video presentation by Navy midshipmen and decided he wanted to go to USNA. However, his guidance counselor discouraged him, saying, "Pete, you should try to be something more reasonable; don't you know Negroes can't go to the Naval Academy?" But Tzomes was not deterred. In 1963, when 250,000 individuals joined Dr. King for the March on Washington, Midshipman Tzomes reported to the Academy. He would go on to become the first African American to command a submarine.

At USNA, Tzomes was one of only twelve blacks in a student population of approximately 4,500.[267] While on a submarine cruise during his senior year, he was overwhelmed by the acceptance of the crew and the support they gave him. However, at the end of the cruise, the Key West Chamber of Commerce sponsored a party for the midshipmen, inviting ladies from the local community to attend. The word was relayed to his CO that Midshipman Tzomes was specifically NOT invited to the party. On hearing about this, the crew of the submarine became upset—and vocal about it. The XO went to the CO, pleading that he should fight for the midshipman, as Tzomes he had done an excellent job and was just as deserving of recognition as any of his classmates. The CO essentially told the XO to stay out of it. However, the XO felt so strongly that he bypassed the CO and went to the squadron commander to complain. Eventually, the XO lost the argument, but his passion taught Midshipman Tzomes a valuable lesson: it's ok to fight for what is right.

Tzomes' most challenging time came when he volunteered for the engineering officer billet on a fast-attack nuclear submarine. While he was underway, his wife went to the first social gathering with the other officers' wives. After greetings were exchanged, the CO's wife told Mrs. Tzomes, "You sure are pretty for a [N-word]. My last experience with a [N-word] was my mammy when I was growing up." Needless to say, Tzomes' wife was not pleased, but he was unable to console her because he was underway and submerged.

As the engineer on board, Tzomes worked extremely hard, but after two weeks, he recalled, his CO told him, "Engineer, I just can't deal with you." Fortunately, the submarine was submerged on a classified mission. Tzomes is sure that if that had not been so, he would have been released from the submarine immediately. However, by the end of the patrol Tzomes had succeeded in completely changing his CO's opinion of him, and was even ranked above the XO in the command—when Tzomes was promoted to the same rank as the serving XO, the CO awarded him a higher precedence, which was unprecedented. This taught Tzomes another valuable lesson: individuals will often recognize competence despite bias. He eventually earned a reputation as "the best engineer in the West," and worked for the Nuclear Propulsion Examining Board prior to assuming command of USS *Houston*.[268]

Rear Admiral Anthony Watson

Background

Anthony Watson was born on the north side of Chicago, in the Cabrini-Green public housing community, in 1949. He grew up in an underserved environment, but always tended to think beyond his current circumstances. A mentor once communicated to Watson an important perspective: "Anthony, it's not in *spite* of growing up in Cabrini-Green that you made it, it's *because* you grew up in Cabrini-Green that you made it. You learned a lot that others never get to experience."

Anthony attended Lane Technical High School and received an appointment to USNA in 1966. (He later would return to the Academy as deputy commandant of midshipmen.) After graduating, he served on six different nuclear submarines, including USS *Jacksonville,* a *Los Angeles*-class fast-attack submarine he commanded.

Watson persevered and triumphed through obstacles, rising to become the first African American flag officer in the submarine force. He went on to work for the Joint Staff under Chairman Colin Powell and commanded the Navy Recruiting Command and its team of over 6000 personnel nationwide.

Significant Operational, Policy, and Technical Contributions

Commanding Officer, USS Jacksonville *(SSN 699)*

Watson and his team conducted the first at-sea, live-fire depth charge tests since those involving USS *Thresher* (SSN 593) in 1963, and the values recorded continue to be used to calculate submarine design thresholds today. His impressive leadership style motivated his crew, and he expertly managed seven different external organizations to complete the project on time and millions of dollars under budget. In spite of the severity of the shock and personnel hazards, he directed damage control efforts to ensure that no personnel injuries occurred, and he maintained his ship in optimal battle-ready status.[269]

Watson improved retention from 39 percent to 92 percent in only eighteen months. He accomplished a very challenging task while developing a motivated team, resulting in a ship that was capable of winning in tactical combat at sea.

Commander, Submarine Squadron 7

Captain Watson's outstanding leadership ability, tactical skill, and initiative contributed to four successful major submarine deployments and operations of strategic importance to the United States. His close supervision of two depot modernization periods and two submarine deactivations was instrumental in those ships successfully completing this difficult evolution while improving the processes for future operations. He spearheaded major quality-of-life improvements for the Pacific submarine force. To ensure the deckplate sailor's interests were considered in every policy change, he spent time with the crew of each of the thirteen ships assigned.

Watson also implemented new roles for attack submarines, and he was instrumental in the formulation of plans and initiatives to respond to changing world commitments.[270]

Deputy Director for Operations, National Military Command Center, the Joint Staff

Rear Admiral Watson's outstanding performance and leadership greatly enhanced the effectiveness of the National Military Command System. His extensive knowledge of worldwide C2 capabilities, emergency action procedures, and the political-military situation resulted in timely and effective coordination with military and civilian decision makers at the highest level of government. He effectively assisted in implementing U.S. policy during critical operations in Somalia, Bosnia, Iraq, Rwanda, Cuba, and Haiti.[271]

Dr. William F. Bundy

Background

William Bundy, the oldest of three siblings, was born in Baltimore, Maryland, in 1946 to William and Paulyne Bundy. He was reared in an environment heavily influenced by his mother and the civil rights era. William attended public schools, including Booker T. Washington Junior High School and Baltimore City College, prior to enlisting in the Navy in 1964.

William's introduction to the Navy was through the U.S. Naval Sea Cadets program, and with his mother's permission he became a part of the Naval Reserve during the summer before his junior year of high school. He was committed to self-improvement, and while serving as an enlisted submarine sonar technician on USS *Sturgeon* and at the Naval Submarine Training Center Pacific, he pursued his college education, eventually earning his Bachelor of Arts degree, with distinction, in liberal studies (technical journalism) from the University of Hawaii.

Bundy attended OCS, graduating first in his class in February 1975, followed by the Submarine Officer Basic Course. He was assigned to the staff of Commander, Submarine Force U.S. Atlantic Fleet prior to completing the Polaris Weapons System Officer training course. Throughout the remainder of his career, Dr. Bundy served in a variety of submarine, surface warfare, and staff assignments that enabled him to leave lasting impacts on the sea services.

Then-Ensign Bundy commenced his submarine officer career during the Cold War era. He served in several nuclear and diesel-electric submarines and on submarine staffs: USS *Sturgeon*, USS *Sam Houston* (Gold), USS *Richard B. Russell*, USS *Memphis*, staff of the U.S. Atlantic Command Nuclear Operations—CTF 144, USS *Lafayette* (Blue), USS *Blueback,* and staff of Submarine Group 5.

Bundy progressed through submarine officer assignments, including assistant weapons officer, electronic materiel officer, combat systems officer, staff nuclear operations officer, operations officer, XO, submarine group plans officer, and ultimately CO of USS *Barbel.* Following his command tour, then-Commander Bundy served as chief staff officer in Submarine Squadron 3; attended the Naval War College, earning a Master of Arts degree with distinction in national security and strategic studies; and served as the director of Naval OCS. He retired from active duty in September 1994. During his thirty-year career, Dr. Bundy rose from being a seaman on the destroyer escort USS *Darby* to the rank of commander.

Then-Lt. Cdr. William F. Bundy and USS *Barbel* officers and crew photographed at Naval Support Facility Sasebo, Japan

U.S. Navy/Public Released

During Dr. Bundy's career as one of about thirty African American officers aboard submarines, he relied on the mentorship of officers in his wardrooms and staffs and on members of NNOA, who were directly and indirectly successors of Vice Admiral Samuel L. Gravely—part of the Gravely legacy. Bundy was a close friend of Captain Pete Tzomes, the first African American submarine CO, and Bundy shared his own experiences with now-Vice Admiral Bruce Grooms and Vice Admiral Mel Williams (Ret.), both of whom, with Dr. Bundy, were members of the Centennial Seven.

William F. Bundy, professor and director of the Gravely Naval Warfare Research Group at the Naval War College, welcomes participants to a Future Surface Combatant workshop held at the Naval War College in Newport, Rhode Island

In 1993, then-Commander Bundy was awarded the Black Engineer of the Year Award for Career Achievement in Government in recognition of his rise from the enlisted ranks to become a submarine CO, and for being an exemplary role model for sailors and officers in the Navy. He also received the 1994 U.S. Navy League Dalton L. Baugh Award for Inspirational Leadership.

When asked about challenging times aboard his submarines or on staff duty, Dr. Bundy responded, "Individuals who were prejudiced were in the minority or were held in check by advances in race relations instituted by Admiral Elmo Zumwalt in the 1970s. His Z-Grams and programs to address race-based bias in the Navy led to my opportunity to become a commissioned officer. Lingering individual prejudice remained, but my opportunities in the Navy were far better than opportunities available to African Americans in communities across the nation."

Dr. Bundy earned the doctor of philosophy degree at Salve Regina University while serving in a leadership role in the private sector before returning to the Naval War College in a faculty position.[272]

Significant Operational, Policy, and Technical Contributions

Staff Officer, Nuclear Operations, Commander Task Force 144, U.S. Atlantic Command

Lieutenant Bundy showcased his technical innovation and his determination in developing and operationalizing certain nuclear targeting data management and C2 capabilities for strategic and tactical nuclear forces.[273]

The strategic submarine force is still using today the procedures that Lieutenant Bundy operationalized in 1982. The author, a former strategic weapons officer on a ballistic-missile submarine, can attest to the significance of these classified procedures, including their contributions to the submarine's strategic warfare capabilities and their vital role in deterring war.

Staff, Commander Submarine Group 5

As plans officer under Commander, Submarine Group 5, Lieutenant Commander Bundy significantly contributed to joint operations by including submarines in combined-arms naval warfare. Prior to this time, submarines had operated largely as independent steamers; Bundy's innovative and creative thinking led to the integration of submarines into combined-arms sea-control operations.[274]

Director, Naval Officer Candidate School

Commander Bundy's determination to offer opportunities for Navy careers to women and minorities extended to OCS, where he personally developed academic standards and teaching approaches that reduced attrition rates. He also instituted ethics and leadership education. He was instrumental in facilitating the transition of the BOOST program on its transfer from San Diego to Newport.[275]

Director, Halsey Charlie and the Gravely Research Group, U.S. Naval War College

Dr. Bundy's ability to innovate and inspire colleagues and students made the College a premier institution of military innovation. The ballistic missile defense (BMD) concept of operations (CONOPS) was developed and implemented through Dr. Bundy's leadership at the College. Dr. Bundy led the Commander, Third Fleet/Commander, Fleet Forces Command effort to respond to CNO direction to develop and employ the Navy's BMD CONOPS. He then led a series of integrated air and missile defense (IAMD) war games, workshops, and concept-development efforts that integrated joint BMD and IAMD capabilities that are still in place today.

Dr. Bundy also created CONOPS for the initial employment of the Navy's *Ohio*-class guided-missile submarines and undersea unmanned vehicles. He directed the Gravely Research Group as it educated War College students to think creatively about maritime, air, and information-dominance warfare.

In addition to his military decorations and service awards, Dr. Bundy was awarded the Navy Civilian Superior Service Medal for his service in directing Navy and joint warfare innovation. He served as the only African American prior-service civilian faculty member at the U.S. Naval War College for more than ten years.[276]

Vice Admiral Melvin G. Williams Jr.

Background

Melvin Williams Jr. was born in November 1955, just one month prior to Rosa Parks' arrest for not giving up her seat on a bus in Montgomery, Alabama.[277] From his birth, his parents, Dora Ruth Williams and Melvin G. Williams Sr., instilled in Melvin the traits of integrity, determination, humility, and servant leadership.

Melvin experienced a character-building moment early in life when he was initially rejected from USNA. He enlisted in the Navy, attended NAPS, and eventually gained entrance to and in 1978 graduated from USNA, with merit, with a Bachelor of Science degree in mathematics. Williams went on to accomplish several "firsts" for an African American in the Navy, such as being the first to command a strategic ballistic-missile submarine, reach the rank of vice admiral, and command the Second Fleet.

Williams' nearly ten years in command included being a submarine commander (USS *Nebraska* [SSBN 739], Gold), a submarine group commander, a submarine squadron commander, and a fleet commander (130 ships and over 90,000 sailors and Marines) during the fleet's HADR response following the devastating earthquake in Haiti in January 2010.

Other key assignments included being XO of *Louisville* during initial combat operations in 1991 during Operation DESERT STORM; chief of staff for the *Kitty Hawk* aircraft carrier strike group during initial combat operations of Operation ENDURING FREEDOM following the September 11th attacks on the nation; director of global operations at USSTRATCOM; and deputy commander, U.S. Fleet Forces.[278]

Significant Operational, Policy, and Technical Contributions

Cruise Missile Staff Officer, Defense Mapping Agency

As a Navy lieutenant assigned to headquarters, Defense Mapping Agency (DMA, now known as the National Geospatial Intelligence Agency), Williams' role was to work with the military services and the combatant commander staffs to develop requirements for the DMA to "digitize" the portions of the world where the developing capability of the newly created Tomahawk cruise missile could be employed in the cause of national defense and security. Lieutenant Williams led the successful effort under which the requirements were generated and the DMA completed its digitization of the earth's topography. His creative and immediate grasp of the cartographic and geodetic sciences enabled him to become an outstanding manager of the Navy's cruise missile mapping, charting, and geodetic require-ments. In 1984, the DMA recognized Lieutenant Williams as one of its "DMA personnel of the year" and awarded him the Defense Meritorious Service Medal for his contributions to the development of the Tomahawk cruise missile's applicability on nuclear submarines, and the DMA itself was awarded the Joint Meritorious Unit Commendation.[279] Later, Williams operationalized this work while serving as XO of *Louisville*.

Engineer Officer, USS Woodrow Wilson *(SSBN 642, Gold)*

Lieutenant Commander Williams and his team developed outstanding training pro-grams; the submarine was awarded the Engineering "E" and the Battle Efficiency "E" for excellence, the Golden Anchor for top retention and programs that care for people, and the Meritorious Unit Commendation. On two occasions, Williams' innovation and strong leadership allowed the ship to meet important underway patrol commitments despite serious last-minute materiel casualties that threatened the mission.[280]

Executive Officer, USS Louisville *(SSN 724)*

Commander Williams was XO of *Louisville* when it made history in January 1991 by becoming the first U.S. nuclear submarine to conduct combat firings, launching the initial strikes during Operation DESERT STORM. When the boat was put on notice to set up an attack posture in December 1990, the CO, Commander Williams, and the crew used their keen judgment and innovative efforts to enable the submarine to travel 14,000 nautical miles at record speed from San Diego to the Red Sea. As the training officer as well as the XO, Williams, with his team, used innovative and creative ways to prepare the crew for its history-making role.[281] The submarine was awarded the Battle Efficiency "E" for excellence and the Navy Unit Commendation.

Commanding Officer, USS Nebraska *(SSBN 739, Gold)*

Williams' Blue-crew counterpart, Commander Bill Hendrickson, and Williams had the privilege of being two of the first officers of commander rank (O-5) to be assigned to command an *Ohio*-class strategic ballistic-missile (Trident) submarine, in 1994. Since the introduction of the class in the early 1980s, these boats had been designated a major command and assigned to second-tour officers of captain rank (O-6). As junior com-manders newly arrived on the waterfront in Kings Bay, Georgia—among the captains who commanded the other submarines—Commanders Hendrickson and Williams assumed command of their crews (designated Blue and Gold, respectively); Williams thereby became the first African American to command a strategic ballistic-missile submarine.

The crews of Nebraska demonstrated extraordinary teamwork from 1994 to 1997. They formed the top-performing strategic missile unit in the nation in 1996. During Williams' first patrol, the ship was tasked, on short notice, to shoot two Trident D5 missiles that had been reconfigured with test systems. This operational test was successful.

During five patrols, Nebraska's Gold crew (teaming with the Blue crew) accomplished the following: Battle Efficiency "E" award for excellence; community service awards and retention awards for service and for taking care of people; Outstanding Ballistic Missile Submarine in the Atlantic Fleet; Navy Meritorious Unit Commendation; and the Omaha trophy as the top strategic missile unit in the nation, in competition with all Navy strategic submarines and all Air Force strategic missile units.[282]

Executive Assistant to Director, Submarine Warfare

As the principal adviser to the director, Captain Williams was instrumental in optimizing submarine force modernization and war-fighting readiness across a forty-five-billion-dollar Future Years Defense Plan. He creatively coordinated monumental staff efforts, leading to the authorization of the first four new attack submarines in the late 1990s, the first Seawolf-class attack submarine, and the naming of the Virginia-class attack submarines.[283]

Commander, Submarine Squadron 4

Captain Williams was responsible for the training, maintenance, and operational readiness of six fast-attack submarines and the support of their crews and families. One of his deployed submarines fired Tomahawk cruise missiles against adversaries in two different combatant commander theaters.[284] The ship later became the first submarine in history to win the Battenberg Cup, which recognizes the best ship in the Atlantic Fleet. Notably, only ships that have been awarded the Battle Efficiency "E" compete for the award; eligible units include aircraft carriers, other surface ships, and submarines.[285]

Chief of Staff, Kitty Hawk Carrier Strike Group

Williams demonstrated his leadership abilities while serving as second in command of the carrier strike group. Following the attacks of September 11th, the strike group received a short-notice mission assignment to the Arabian Sea. Williams creatively applied lessons from his days aboard Louisville ten years earlier. This mission was highly successful—the opening act of Operation ENDURING FREEDOM. The Kitty Hawk group was awarded the Meritorious Unit Commendation. Captain Williams' innovative ability to inspire and lead people contributed to his team's success.[286]

Commander, Submarine Group 9

Williams led the successful training, maintenance, and operations of twenty-four commands for over two years. This included successful strategic deterrence patrols, maintenance on assigned fast-attack submarines, and conversion of *Ohio* and *Michigan* from strategic ballistic-missile nuclear submarines (SSBNs) into guided-missile nuclear submarines (SSGNs). SSGN capabilities included carrying over a hundred Tomahawk cruise missiles. This capability was actuated in conflict in 2012 during Operation ODYSSEY DAWN in Libya. Williams and his team also validated the first D-5 missile test capability in the Pacific theater, which established the full Trident II D-5 strategic deterrent capabilities, then oversaw the successful completion of forty successful strategic deterrence patrols by Trident SSBNs.[287]

Atlantic Ocean, 20 July 2009. Commander, U.S. Second Fleet Vice Adm. Mel Williams Jr. speaks to Lt. (j.g.) Byron Stocks on the navigation bridge of aircraft carrier USS *Carl Vinson* (CVN 70) as Stocks stands watch as OOD. *Carl Vinson* was conducting flight deck certification.

U.S. Navy photo by Mass Communication Specialist 3rd Class Joshua Nistas/Released

Commander, Second Fleet

In 2006, Williams became the sixth African American in the Navy's 235-year history to reach vice admiral rank, and the first African American submarine-qualified officer in history to reach three stars. He immediately served as deputy commander, U.S. Fleet Forces.

In 2008, Williams became Commander, U.S. Second Fleet, the first African American to command a fleet. Vice Admiral Williams' innovative and creative leadership contributed to his team's efficient and effective response with HADR to Galveston, Texas, after the destructive Hurricane Ike, and again during HADR to Haiti following a devastating 7.0 earthquake.

Additionally, one of the ships that had been trained and certified for deployment—including counterpiracy operations—was USS *Bainbridge*. *Bainbridge* contributed to the heroic rescue of Captain Phillips of MV *Maersk Alabama*. In his concurrent role as NATO support director, Combined Joint Operations from the Sea Center of Excellence, Williams' team contributed to the first-ever, CJCS-produced NATO counterpiracy tactics and an alliance maritime strategy.[288]

Admiral Cecil D. Haney

Background

Cecil Haney hails from the Washington, DC, area. His mother was employed as a seamstress and his father as a taxicab driver; the latter also worked at the Greyhound bus terminal, first as a janitor, retiring as a ticket salesman. Although his parents were not college educated, they were huge proponents of education. During his high school years, Cecil worked through the summers, and it was understood early that he had to pay for his college education.

Haney was exposed to computer programming while working at Naval Sea Systems Command during his summer breaks, and he had the opportunity to visit various laboratories, which gave him an early appreciation for engineering. Initially he had wanted to become a medical doctor, but after realizing that he did not have enough money saved to make it through college, he shifted his goal to Army service; however, a Navy captain he met with at Naval Sea Systems Command convinced him to consider the Navy. Cecil applied to and was accepted at USNA, and graduated in 1978.

During his early Navy years, Haney became active in the Navy's Blue and Gold program, conducting final interviews as part of the nomination and application process for entry to the Academy.[289]

Significant Operational, Policy, and Technical Contributions

Radiological Controls Officer, Repair Department, USS Frank Cable (AS 40)

Lieutenant Haney's astute leadership, impressive managerial abilities, and ingenuity maintained his division at maximum efficiency for Commander, Submarine Squadron 4.[290] It should be noted that even when Haney was just a young Navy lieutenant, people commonly used words such as *inspirational, enthusiastic,* and *innovative* to describe him.

Engineer Officer, USS Hyman G. Rickover (SSN 709)

Lieutenant Commander Haney's innovative, direct, and personal involvement in extensive nuclear repair modifications ensured this nuclear asset was rapidly returned to the front line of action after being sidelined by an untimely need for repairs.[291]

Commanding Officer, USS Honolulu (SSN 718) and Special Operations

Haney's creativity and innovation led his ship to achieve the highest grades in all inspections, and his dedication to his crew and ship led to his selection for the 1998 Vice Admiral Stockdale Leadership Award.[292]

Appropriations Liaison Officer, Under Secretary of Defense (Comptroller), Washington, DC

Captain Haney's exceptional knowledge of the DoD budget, combined with his outstanding ability to understand and interpret the congressional process, contributed significantly to the mission of the Under Secretary. Haney found ingenious ways to keep senior advisers to the Secretary of Defense updated on vital policy matters. Haney made invaluable contributions to the department's success in obtaining funding for research-and-development programs that protected the superiority of America's fighting forces.[293]

Commander, Submarine Squadron 1

Haney's personal involvement and endless energy challenged his COs during their deployment training cycles to ensure crew readiness for support of numerous national missions. His creativity in improving formal structures for developing and certifying joint submarine and naval special warfare capability associated with the Dry Deck Shelter operation and the Advanced SEAL Delivery System was unprecedented. It was because of Captain Haney's commendable innovation and diligent efforts that the first deployment of this transformational technology succeeded with impressive results.[294]

Director, Submarine Warfare

Rear Admiral Haney's innovation and creativity ensured the successful initiation of the *Ohio*-class submarine replacement program, which guaranteed the Navy's ability to maintain a continuous sea-based strategic deterrent capability. The hundred-billion-dollar program became the standard bearer and model for cost reductions and efficiency. His creativity was instrumental in the successful progression of the *Virginia*-class program that resulted in a doubling of the annual build rate—one of the Navy's most successful shipbuilding programs.[295]

Deputy Chief, Plans and Policies, U.S. Pacific Fleet

In an assignment involving considerable accountability and responsibility, Admiral Haney brought innovation and creativity to several initiatives, including staff realignment and consolidation of plans and policies that streamlined planning and added considerable strategic value to the fleet as a whole. His efforts were critical to Pacific Fleet's effective and timely provision of support to the combatant commander. Admiral Haney planned the USNS *Mercy* (T-AH 19) HADR deployment following one of the worst tsunami disasters in history.[296]

Admiral Haney returned to assume command of Pacific Fleet in January 2012. He orchestrated one of the largest RIMPACs, involving numerous allies and partner nations. He also deployed the first littoral combat ship to the Pacific, in addition to deploying numerous aircraft carrier strike groups to the PACOM and CENTCOM areas of responsibility.[297]

Commander, U.S. Strategic Command

USSTRATCOM is one of the country's nine combatant commands. As its commander, Vice Admiral Haney fully implemented one of the first significant changes to the Unified Command Plan since 2002. His innovation and creativity led the successful effort to help U.S. Cyber Command integrate its effects into every combatant command worldwide. He led the command through Operations TOMADACHI AND ODYSSEY DAWN, integrating unprecedented global-strike options and space support and combating weapons of mass destruction resources.[298]

Vice Admiral Bruce E. Grooms

Background

Bruce Grooms was born in Cleveland, Ohio, and was raised in the small town of Maple Heights. He was one of four siblings born into a working-class family with humble beginnings. His father was a postal worker; his mother was a dedicated homemaker and a devout Christian. Grooms' family did not have many material possessions, but any such lack was compensated for by an abundance of love. So he understood at a very early age that he was, above all else, dearly loved, and was encouraged to be the best at whatever he set his mind to accomplish.

Following high school, Grooms attended USNA, graduating in 1980 with a degree in aerospace engineering; he was also the captain of the varsity basketball team and was selected for nuclear power training.

After completing the nuclear training pipeline, Grooms reported to his first submarine, USS *Jacksonville*. Aware that he was one of very few African American submarine officers, he was pleasantly surprised to receive a change-of-command invitation from Captain Pete Tzomes, the first African American to command a submarine. This developed into a lasting mentoring relationship that helped Grooms keep himself balanced throughout the challenging years ahead.[299]

Significant Operational, Policy, and Technical Contributions

Company Officer/Commandant of Midshipmen, USNA

Bruce Grooms demonstrated promise as a young lieutenant. During his tour as a company officer at the Academy, he practiced sound leadership techniques and presented the highest example of integrity, responsibility, and accountability. He creatively upgraded the summer cruise manual, which enhanced the quality of training for future Navy and Marine Corp officers. He innovatively developed a meaningful exit questionnaire to study female attrition at the Academy as part of the work of the Women's Advisory Committee—diversity of the sea services was a priority for him from the very beginning.[300]

Later, Vice Admiral Grooms was selected to be the first African American commandant of midshipmen at the Academy, responsible for the training, professional development, and day-to-day activities of the 4,500 midshipmen in the brigade. In this capacity, he was the equivalent of the dean of students at a civilian university.[301]

Executive Officer, USS Pasadena *(SSN 752)/Commanding Officer,*
USS Asheville *(SSN 758)*

While serving as XO of *Pasadena*, Grooms demonstrated a talent for creative and innovative warfare, executing extremely successful operations in the unforgiving, shallow waters of the Arabian Gulf. As command duty officer, he oversaw significant operations that were of vital importance to the security of the United States.[302] While serving as CO of *Asheville*, he displayed superior tactical expertise and creativity in guiding his ship through a tremendously successful western Pacific deployment. His command was evaluated as the best in the squadron in all areas, including engineering, tactics, and retention. His submarine was awarded the Battle Efficiency "E" for overall superior performance.

His submarine also won the Golden Anchor award for having the highest retention in the submarine force. His innovative methods of improving the quality of life for his sailors and their families provided the command with the highest levels of morale and job satisfaction in the squadron.[303] Grooms was selected as the 1999 winner of the Admiral Stockdale Leadership Award for his inspirational leadership while serving in command.[304]

Senior Inspector, Nuclear Propulsion Examining Board (NPEB)

Admiral Grooms was the first African American to serve as the senior inspector of the NPEB. He displayed extraordinary professional skill, resourcefulness, and inspired leadership. He integrated uncompromising examination standards to complement changing operational requirements. His insightful analysis and solution-oriented feedback improved fleet readiness and continued the legacy of safety for nuclear-powered submarines, surface ships, and support facilities in the Atlantic Fleet.[305]

Senior Military Aide to the Under Secretary of Defense for Policy

As the principal military adviser to the under secretary, he was responsible for the coordination and execution of all defense policy and national security matters under the purview of the under secretary. His role was to help facilitate the gathering of responsive, forward-thinking, and insightful policy advice to support the Secretary of Defense. Present in the Pentagon during the fateful September 11th attack, he was instrumental in assisting the under secretary in developing and adapting plans and policy in the immediate aftermath of the attacks.[306]

Commander, Submarine Squadron 6

Captain Grooms was responsible for the training, maintenance, operations, and deployment certification of eight fast-attack submarines and two strategic ballistic-missile submarines undergoing conversion to guided-missile nuclear submarines. Captain Grooms made significant contributions to the nation's combat readiness and operational prowess, ensuring the nuclear-powered submarines under his care were ready to accomplish their missions at a moment's notice. Specifically, his attention to detail, high standards, and total involvement were key attributes of the Atlantic submarine force's best-run fast-attack submarines. He innovatively prepared his team of submarine captains to push their commands beyond expectations. He ensured all methods used to test the submarines were challenging, realistic, and very closely matched wartime conditions. Captain Grooms' inspirational leadership fostered the development of sailors who were dedicated to the mission and contributed to very high retention rates in the U.S. Navy.[307]

Director, Submarine Warfare Division

Admiral Grooms' financial innovation and creativity was the bedrock beneath his exceptional stewardship of the undersea warfare program. He managed a budget of more than ten billion dollars per year, and seventy-eight billion across the Future Years Defense Plan. During his tenure, three *Virginia*-class fast-attack submarines and two *Ohio*-class guided-missile submarines achieved significant milestones, including the initial operating capability certification of the *Virginia*-class boat and the first-ever deployment of a submarine with cruise missiles aboard. Admiral Grooms was instrumental in the decision to increase the procurement rate for the *Virginia*-class fast-attack submarine program to two per year in FY 2011.[308] He was also instrumental in the initial planning and development of the *Ohio*-class ballistic-missile submarine replacement program.[309]

Commander, Submarine Group 2

Admiral Grooms ensured that, for all aspects of training, maintenance, operations, and deployment certifications, all thirty fast-attack submarines in the Atlantic Fleet were second to none. Additionally, he provided oversight for all *Virginia*-class submarines undergoing new construction, including sea trials, tests, and evaluations prior to delivery to the Navy. This program has been hailed as the best ship-production program in the twenty-first century.

    As the operational commander for all thirty east coast fast-attack submarines, Grooms' inspirational leadership and exceptional command philosophy led to peak operational readiness across the waterfront. Possessing strategic vision and persistence, he effectively ensured that efforts to meet the critical challenges facing the submarine forces—such as new construction of the *Virginia*-class submarine, outfitting of current submarines, and protection of deployed forces—were managed properly and completed successfully. A leader who is passionate about personal and professional growth, Admiral Grooms' mentoring efforts left a lasting impact on the next generation of submariners.[310]

Vice Director, Joint Staff

Admiral Grooms was directly responsible to the CJCS to manage all aspects of the Joint Staff, including administering the budget and finance, executing all responsibilities of the chief information officer, and managing all staff resource plans and information security programs for the more than 2000 civilian and military members of the staff.

Grooms spearheaded efforts to improve DoD and interagency collaboration dramatically so as to shape concepts that define the future conduct of joint and combined operations. He played an influential role in the chairman's strategic reviews that directly enhanced the security and welfare of our nation and its allies. He creatively orchestrated the Secretary of Defense's senior executive service efficiency efforts that aligned with the executive branch's domestic economic mandate while skillfully defending Joint Staff equities.[311]

Assistant Deputy CNO, Plans/Policy

Admiral Grooms' innovative and transformational leadership directly supported operations around the world, including Operations TOMODACHI, NEW DAWN, and UNIFIED PROTECTOR. As the CNO's lead for the air-sea battle concept, he creatively implemented efforts to develop this new operational concept through personal involvement in joint forums. His efforts were critical to advancing the implementation of the air-sea battle concept, the strategic centerpiece of U.S. Navy modernization efforts.[312]

Captain Joseph P. Peterson

Background

Captain Peterson is a native of Bluemont, Virginia, and was one of six children born to Lavenia and Theodore Peterson. During his adolescent years he performed landscape duties for the former U.S. senator from Virginia, John Warner.

Peterson served for eight years as an enlisted electronics technician prior to obtaining his bachelor's degree in economics from Rollins College. He received his commission in 1980 via OCS. His sea duty assignments included serving aboard USS *Mariano G. Vallejo* (SSBN 658) (twice), USS *John C. Calhoun* (SSBN 630), and USS *Dolphin* (AGSS 555)—in the latter serving as both XO and CO.[313]

Dolphin was, at the time, the Navy's only operational diesel-electric, deep-diving research-and-development submarine. It conducted various important missions for the Navy that led to significant milestones in innovation and creativity.[314]

After his command tour, Captain Peterson reported to Commander, Naval Sea Systems Command in Washington, DC. Captain Peterson retired in July 2013 as senior program manager for American Systems Corporation at the Washington Navy Yard.[315]

Significant Operational, Policy, and Technical Contributions

*Member, Weapons Operations, Test, and Evaluation Branch, Technical Division,
Strategic Systems Program, Washington, DC*

Captain Peterson served in the Navy during the height of the Cold War. One can argue
that the United States was victorious because it outspent and outsmarted the Soviets
with respect to designing and manufacturing nuclear weapons. Captain Peterson played
a major role in the design and development of the Trident II SLBMs that are currently
on board U.S. ballistic-missile submarines. His contributions led directly to increased
accuracy, greater payload capability, and significant evaluation metrics for the nation's
most formidable nuclear deterrent weapon.[316]

*Senior Liaison/Project Officer/Major Program Manager, Program Executive Office,
Submarines, Washington, DC*

Captain Peterson brilliantly developed and transitioned a successful first-time program
that replaced the combat system on Australia's *Collins*-class submarine with a U.S. combat system. His creativity as program manager fulfilled a presidential directive to deliver
diesel-electric submarines to Taiwan. This politically sensitive submarine acquisition
program was at the time the largest U.S. foreign military sale. Captain Peterson also
contributed significantly to the design and development of the first nuclear-powered
guided-missile submarine, and to overcoming funding shortfalls for procurement.[317]

SPECIAL RECOGNITION: THE HEART OF COMMAND AND SENIOR LEADERSHIP

Rear Admiral Lawrence Chambers was the first African American USNA graduate to achieve flag officer rank. He also has a unique story to share about his involvement with the end of the Vietnam War. The Honorable B. J. "Buddie" Penn was appointed acting Secretary of the Navy, the highest position an African American has held in the department. He is a retired naval aviator who had a unique and compelling life journey through the Navy and the halls of the Pentagon. This special recognition section is devoted to Chambers and Penn.

Rear Admiral Lawrence C. Chambers

Background

Lawrence Chambers was born in Bedford, Virginia, but grew up in the Washington, DC, area. His father died when he was very young, which left his mother to take care of him and his four siblings on an office worker's salary.

From early on, Chambers aspired to become an engineer or a pilot. He pursued this dream by enrolling in JROTC in high school. As high school drew to a close, he approached the USNA midshipman who would become the first African American to graduate from that institution, Wesley Brown Jr., and inquired about attending himself. Chambers became the second African American to graduate from USNA.

Upon commissioning in 1952, Chambers reported to Pensacola, Florida, for flight training—and an illustrious career ensued. Both he and his brother Andrew ascended to executive levels in the services: Andrew retired as a lieutenant general in the U.S. Army and Lawrence retired as a rear admiral.

Captain Chambers took command of USS *Midway* (CV 41) on March 25, 1975, and the ship got underway from Yokosuka, Japan, on March 31, heading to the Arabian Sea. The plan was to conduct flight operations to get the pilots and crews back up to speed, since the ship had been in port for thirty-three days. But within the first week of taking command, the new captain would be tested.

Midway's combat information center reported a skunk [a new surface radar contact] 35,000 yards east of the ship's position. At 16,000 yards, the signal bridge identified the skunk as a Russian warship. As the two vessels approached each other, Captain Chambers signaled that he was conducting flight operations and was restricted in his ability to maneuver. The Russian vessel did not respond. From his experience operating in this region, Chambers knew that Russian warships often ignored signals from American vessels.

As the ships continued to close, the OOD determined that the Russian warship was on a steady bearing with decreasing range, that is, on a collision course. Slowly the Russian ship's bearing started to drift to the right, and the vessel crossed *Midway*'s bow at a range of 6000 yards. Then the Russian vessel turned 180 degrees and went dead in the water—directly ahead of *Midway*. The Russian ship immediately ran up the international signal for "not under command"—which normally indicates a loss of power.

Just then, one of *Midway*'s pilots radioed that he was experiencing an emergency and needed to make an emergency landing on the flight deck. The situation on the bridge was getting increasingly tense. *Midway* continued her steady course and speed, while the Russian warship performed no maneuvering to clear the bow.

Captain Chambers asked the OOD, "Would you mind if I take the conn for a while?" Any instance of the captain of a warship taking the conn is very significant, because responsibility for any ensuing actions, good or bad, then resides fully with the CO personally. With a sigh of relief, the OOD relinquished the conn to Captain Chambers. Chambers gave only one order: "Steer nothing to the right of 135 degrees." This would indeed be a game of chicken. The bridge became very quiet. When *Midway* drew within 3000 yards of the Russian warship, the other vessel immediately hauled down its breakdown flag and maneuvered to get off *Midway*'s projected track. The Russian vessel passed safely about 300 yards down *Midway*'s port side. The OOD asked, "Captain, when were you going to maneuver to avoid the collision?" The captain smiled and replied, "You have the conn."

Since the Russians "kept book" on all U.S. carrier skippers, Chambers had no problems with Russian warships after this incident; they always observed the rules of the road when USS *Midway* was in the vicinity.

Shortly after the encounter with the Russian warship, Chambers was ordered to proceed to Okinawa to onload two squadrons of Marine helicopters. After transferring the Marines to USS *Hancock* (CV 19), he was directed to proceed to Subic Bay, the Philippines, for ten days of upkeep—but with a requirement to maintain readiness to get underway within four hours. Two days after entering Subic Bay, he received a message to get underway and make best speed to the southern tip of Vietnam to take aboard ten HH-53 helicopters belonging to U.S. Air Force special operations units. In other words, *Midway* was needed to assist in the evacuation of Saigon.

Best speed for *Midway* meant burning over 750,000 gallons of fuel a day. It was no easy task to get all twelve boilers back online following the upkeep. Although the ship was underway in less than four hours, its engineers required an additional two hours to bring all twelve boilers back on line. *Midway* proceeded to the rendezvous on a flank bell—she was steaming at thirty-two-plus knots. On April 23, 1975, *Midway* arrived on Yankee Station off the coast of South Vietnam. Beyond that, Captain Chambers did not know when he would be ordered to execute the evacuation mission, Operation FREQUENT WIND.

On the morning of April 29, 1975, the vice premier of South Vietnam landed on *Midway*. Later that afternoon, *Midway* received orders to execute FREQUENT WIND. The ship launched the HH-53s. On their return, many people embarked onto the ship, including South Vietnamese citizens and other foreign nationals; security was a concern, and *Midway*'s Marines were authorized to use deadly force to keep order.

On the afternoon of the second day (April 30), Captain Chambers received a note from a Major Buong Ly, who circled the aircraft carrier in a small (two-seat) Cessna O-1 Bird Dog. The note said, "Please move your planes and make room for me. I can land on your runway. I have enough fuel for one hour of flight time. Please rescue me." It was signed "Major Buong Ly wife and 5 children." Major Ly dropped a total of four such notes as he circled above, three of which went overboard. Captain Chambers, however, did not need the note to know what Ly wanted. Ly had no other place to land—he did not have sufficient fuel to return to the beach.

Chambers' administrative immediate superior in command ordered him not to make a ready deck for this aircraft; *Midway*'s flight deck was full of helicopters and people recently evacuated from Vietnam. In fact, the admiral in charge publicly reprimanded the captain over the 21MC when he attempted to make a ready deck to receive the major and his family. When Chambers' bridge crew heard the conflicting orders over the 21MC speakers, he told the crew that he was their CO and they were to do as he directed. Then Chambers phoned the air boss and told him to make a ready deck to receive the plane flying above. The air boss, astounded at this directive, said, "Captain, you gotta be shitting me? I don't have room, and I don't have the manpower." Captain Chambers replied, "Sure you do, and I'm going to help you." Chambers got on the ship's 1MC (the general announcing system) and said to his crew, "I need all red shirts, green shirts, blue shirts, brown shirts, yellow shirts, and white shirts on the flight deck, and on the double!" [Shirt colors signified different crew functions.] Chambers not only got those crewmen on deck; he also got the Marines and everyone else not on watch, including pilots and junior officers.

The CO's order was to make a ready deck for the airplane flying above. He deliberately did not watch the evolution, because he expected to be called to testify later, and he did not want to know any of the details. After the ship's personnel dumped a number of helicopters overboard, another flight of helicopters appeared over the horizon and landed on *Midway's* flight deck without a signal. To clear the landing area, the flight deck crew had to push these helicopters over the side as well. Captain Chambers was very concerned about the landing speed of the Bird Dog, so he called the chief engineer and told him he needed twenty-five knots out of "the Old Girl" to add to the fifteen knots of natural wind. With forty knots of wind over the deck, the pilot would have to carry extra power to handle the turbulence in the ship's wake. It would require exceptional proficiency on the part of the aircraft's pilot to complete the maneuver successfully. To Chambers' relief, the landing was a success. Chambers spoke briefly with Major Ly for three to four minutes. Many years later, they were able to renew their acquaintance.

Later, Captain Chambers asked the chief of staff of the Army for permission for the Navy to keep the airplane; it is now on display at the Naval Air Museum in Pensacola, Florida. In April 2014, the Ly and Chambers families got together during an air expo in Lakeland, Florida, to celebrate the landing on *Midway*. Seven grandchildren were part of the celebration.

Rear Adm. Larry Chambers. "He didn't have to save the family with five small children. He could have let them die; no one would have faulted him for it. Given the chaos that was ensuing all around him, it would have been just another sad footnote crowded into another sad chapter in history, and one quickly forgotten."

Mitch Traphagen, quote and photo.

After *Midway* was done with the refugee business, Captain Chambers was ordered to make a full-power run through the San Bernardino Strait in the Philippines at night. He is proud to say he is the only CO to take an aircraft carrier through this narrow strait at full power under the cloak of darkness. Chambers was ordered to proceed to Guam and offload the helicopters, other aircraft, and refugees and return to the South China Sea because of the ongoing *Mayaguez* incident.

Captain Chambers' courage to do the right thing under intense pressure is inspiring, and his innovative leadership stands as an example for all naval officers to emulate.

However, some conflicts in which Rear Admiral Chambers was involved did not end gloriously. One was Operation EAGLE CLAW, which took place during the Iran hostage crisis. Chambers was commander of the *Coral Sea* battle group. His job was to provide tactical air support for the rescue attempt. The battle group was on station at sea for 110 days before a decision was made to rescue the hostages from Iran. The mission was designed to be conducted on a moonless night during the winter months when there was sufficient darkness to cover the entire mission. But because of the 110-day delay in receiving the order to execute EAGLE CLAW, it was questionable whether the plan could be executed under the cloak of darkness.

Once the decision was made, the CIA set up an intermediate airfield for the helicopters to be refueled en route to Tehran. The operation began, and at first all went well. The helicopters made it to the intermediate airfield and were serviced with fuel. They had enough to make it to the embassy in Tehran, pick up the hostages, and return to the outlying field, where the hostages and their rescuers were to be flown out of Iran in C130 aircraft. The rescue helicopters were to be abandoned at the intermediate airfield.

But while refueling at the intermediate airfield, the on-scene commander observed a series of trucks passing on a nearby road. Those in charge of the task group assumed the rescuers had been discovered, and they decided to abort the mission. At this point the rescue helicopters had only enough fuel to get to Tehran and back to the airfield; they would need more fuel to make the return trip to USS *Enterprise* in the Indian Ocean. Meanwhile, a severe desert sandstorm engulfed the airfield, causing the visibility to drop to near zero. While repositioning the helicopters to obtain more fuel, a helicopter collided with a C-130. Eight American servicemen died in the accident.[318]

Significant Operational, Policy, and Technical Contributions

Air Officer, USS Oriskany *(CVA 34)*

Commander Chambers' air department performed in an exceptionally outstanding manner, contributing significantly to the highly successful combat flights conducted against the enemy in Southeast Asia. He met the stringent demands of tight, crowded schedules with an impressive launching and recovery safety record and still maintained the fast and ready flight deck that was essential to successful combat air operations in Vietnam.[319]

Commanding Officer, USS Midway *(CV 41)*

Captain Chambers demonstrated superior leadership while operating his ship in the unique role of a helicopter carrier for ten U.S. HH-53 helicopters. His command was instrumental in the evacuation of over 3000 Vietnamese, U.S., and third-country nationals from Saigon. In a historic evolution that saved many lives and millions of dollars, he recovered forty-five South Vietnamese UH-1 helicopters, three CH-47 helicopters, and fixed-wing aircraft that were all heavily loaded with refugees. He led the *Midway*/ Carrier Air Wing 5 team to the highest levels of combat readiness despite numerous complexities evolving from sustained arduous deployment and a rigorous employment schedule.[320]

Commander, Carrier Group 3

Admiral Chambers improved operational readiness, tactical procedures, and logistics coordination while commanding carrier battle groups in every operational environment in the Pacific Fleet. The unprecedented level of readiness his battle group maintained during an extended deployment was a direct result of Admiral Chambers' exceptional professional abilities and skillful coordination of all available assets.[321]

The Honorable B. J. "Buddie" Penn

Background

B. J. "Buddie" Penn was born in Peru, Indiana. He had no siblings and was raised in a two-parent home. Although his father possessed only a fourth-grade education and his mother only graduated from high school, his parents were staunch supporters of education and taught him three amazing lessons: whatever you learn no one can take from you; you can accomplish anything in life if you want it badly enough; and no one can make you feel inferior unless you let them. Those lessons served him well throughout his life.

Penn's father worked on the railroad and his mother was a domestic. He often accompanied his parents to their places of business; from this he learned the value of hard work and the benefits of a good education. At an early age, he was fond of airplanes, and his neighbor, who owned a small plane, exposed him to flying. This made a lasting impression on him and instilled a love of flying in his heart.

During Penn's younger years growing up in Indiana, he had to overcome blatant racism. Few people realize that the roots of the Ku Klux Klan—a group infamous for its hatred of and historical use of violence against minorities—can be traced to Indiana. His mother, however, had experienced the Klan even more intimately as a child growing up in Kentucky. During her youth, the "night riders" harassed her family; this eventually caused them to leave the South and move northward to escape harassment. As a small child, Penn remembered viewing a photo of a lynching that had occurred in a small town near Peru. The photo was placed in the window of the drug store on Main Street to serve as a warning to local blacks to remain "in their place."

Yet even though the Klan was prevalent in the area, a silent majority of people supported African Americans. For example, Penn's high school math teacher encouraged him to pursue a college degree. Yet even though Penn delivered newspapers at 4 AM and was prepared for school by 7 AM, then maintained good grades in high school, no one except his math teacher spoke to him about attending college. This teacher was a former submariner and a graduate of Purdue University, and this influenced Penn to attend Purdue. It was a land-grant college, which meant that enrollment in an ROTC program was required. Penn joined the Air Force ROTC unit. However, after graduating, his buddies in the Navy spoke to him about landing on aircraft carriers. This seemed more challenging than landing on a large airfield, so Penn decided to pursue a flying career in the Navy.

At the time, there were fewer than 200 African American officers in the Navy, and they were all relatively junior: the most senior aviator was Lieutenant Louis Williams, the senior African American naval officer was Chaplain Thomas David Parham, the senior African American line officer was Lieutenant Commander Samuel L. Gravely, and the senior Marine officer was Captain Frank Peterson.

After graduating from Purdue, Penn passed the flight exam in Glenview, Illinois, and proceeded to take the commissioning physical in Pensacola, Florida. There he was told two things: that he had not scored high enough on the math portion of the commissioning exam (although he had graduated from Purdue University in three years); and that his rear teeth did not meet well enough. Refusing to allow overt racism to deter him, Penn took the math exam again and had the requisite dental work done—with six teeth pulled—to pass the physical. Then he reported to Pensacola.

During this time, on average only one African American pilot made it through flight school per year—attrition was extremely high. After Penn reported, one of his instructors asked him, "What are you doing here? You want to be the first coon on the moon?" Undeterred by racist comments such as these, Penn graduated from flight school second in his class.

Penn completed junior officer and mid-grade officer assignments. His hard work and aviation skills finally brought him a command opportunity, as an aircraft squadron commander. After commanding the largest aircraft squadron in the Navy, Penn received orders to report to USNA, because the Navy required senior minority leaders to assist in diversity initiatives.

As a battalion officer, Penn was responsible for 1,200 midshipmen. He was also responsible for plebe summer. Historically, after the grueling plebe summer, numerous individuals are sure to resign; but none did so under his leadership.

During this time, the Academy graduated its first female midshipmen, including Michelle Howard, who became Admiral Michelle Howard, Vice CNO. Penn went on to become the special assistant to the CNO for equal opportunity/minority affairs, and was the first and only African American acting Secretary of the Navy.[322]

Rear Adm. Bruce Grooms and Acting Navy Secretary B. J. Penn with Vice Adm. Donnelly

Significant Operational, Policy, and Technical Contributions

Pilot, Tactical Electronic Warfare Squadron 132, USS America *(CVA 66)*

Lieutenant Commander Penn engaged in combat operations while attached to USS *America*. He engaged the adversary in Southeast Asia from July 12, 1972, to January 31, 1973. Flying under hazardous conditions, he successfully completed over 260 combat missions in an active combat area. His cool and calm demeanor under fire exhibited great professionalism and was in keeping with Navy aviation's traditional fighting spirit.[323]

Commanding Officer, Naval Air Station North Island, Coronado, California

Commander Penn displayed extraordinary, innovative leadership skills as he orchestrated a vast array of support elements while saving the Navy millions of dollars. His exceptional management of the Model Installation Program and the futuristic Five Year Plan became fleet models in achieving excellence in innovation.[324]

Special Assistant for Equal Opportunity/Minority Affairs to the CNO

Captain Penn's sage counsel and expertise in minority affairs made him an invaluable confidant for the CNO. He implemented programs (of which the author was a direct beneficiary) that, combined with his expert advice, competence, and dedication, were significant factors that led to successful accomplishment of the Navy's diversity goals. His counsel and thorough knowledge of the Navy's Equal Opportunity Programs were superb in every respect, and his execution of the programs was beyond exceptional, further improving the Navy's image in this very important area.[325] Penn's foundational work provided lasting contributions that built the framework of the Navy's diversity base of today.

Director, Security Assistance Operations for Navy International Programs

Captain Penn's creative brilliance directly impacted the forty-two-billion-dollar Foreign Military Sales program, which directly benefited the Navy, key allies, and the international stature of the United States. His aggressive management style was key in providing one billion dollars in weapons system and logistics support to coalition forces during Operations DESERT SHIELD and DESERT STORM. This support was instrumental to the decisive victories both these campaigns secured. Penn also devised strategies that enabled the Navy to maintain its arsenal of major weapons systems, such as Aegis, Harpoon, F/A-18, and P-3, and their availability for coalition forces. Captain Penn's personal efforts allowed the United States to market and sell military systems and equipment to key countries that at the time were excluded from U.S. markets. This included the implementation of two complex multinational frigate construction programs that were instrumental in revitalizing the Navy's program of ship-leasing to other countries.[326]

CONCLUSION

Nelson Mandela, the first black president of South Africa, once said, "As we let our own light shine, we unconsciously give others permission to do the same." Vice Admiral Samuel Gravely Jr. did not seek the spotlight, but his example inspired others to step into the light of history, leaving a lasting legacy for the entire country.

This legacy includes leadership lessons. Inspirational leadership is a common theme running through these flag officers' stories. This type of leadership motivates others to act positively—to think creatively, work harder at any task, and work toward mission accomplishment—rather than be cowed by fear of reprisal. According to Michael Hyatt in *Four Characteristics of Inspirational Leaders*, "Inspirational leaders help people believe in themselves. . . . Great leaders—like great parents—help people believe in themselves. They look for opportunities to catch people doing something right. They focus on their people's strengths, not their weaknesses. And, they have a knack for offering encouragement at strategic moments—when the team needs it."[327]

This book has highlighted several examples of inspirational and innovative leadership, from the events surrounding Vice Admiral Gravely's contributions to the Defense Satellite Communication Systems, to Rear Admiral Chambers inspiring his team during the evacuation of Saigon, to Vice Admiral Melvin Williams contributing to the foundational principles of the Tomahawk missile program, to Admiral Michelle Howard's role in the rescue of Captain Richard Phillips from Somali pirates. These American patriots continue to keep the light burning for a generation of future trailblazers whose impact will continue to help America maintain its competitive edge in the twenty-first century. Vice Admiral Samuel L. Gravely's legacy of inspiring African American flag officers and other leaders has provided a model that educates, motivates, and strengthens all Americans. May they continue to have fair winds and following seas.

ACRONYMS AND ABBREVIATIONS

Note that some of the terms listed come from different eras, so there may be overlap, and not all are still in use.

AE	ammunition ship (ship type)
AO	fleet oiler (ship type)
AOCS	Aviation Officer Candidate School
AROCS	Aviation Reserve Officer Candidate School
AS	submarine tender (ship type)
ASW	antisubmarine warfare
AVT	auxiliary training carrier (ship type)
BEYA	Black Engineer of the Year Award
BOOST	Broadened Opportunity for Officer Selection and Training
C2	command and control
C3	command, control, and communications
C3I	command, control, communications, and intelligence
C4	command, control, communications, and computers
C4I	command, control, communications, computers, and intelligence
CENTCOM	Central Command
CG	guided-missile cruiser (ship type)
CGN	nuclear-powered guided-missile cruiser (ship type)
CINC	commander in chief
CINCPAC	commander in chief, Pacific
CJCS	Chairman of the Joint Chiefs of Staff (the armed forces' top uniformed officer)
CLG	guided-missile cruiser, light (ship type)
CNET	Commander, Naval Education and Training
CNO	Chief of Naval Operations (the Navy's top uniformed officer)
CO	commanding officer
COMNAVAIRLANT	Commander, Naval Air, Atlantic
COMNAVAIRPAC	Commander, Naval Air, Pacific
COMNAVSURFLANT	Commander, Naval Surface Force, Atlantic Fleet

COMPHIBRON	Commander, amphibious squadron ___
conn	Short for "conning." The conning officer is legally responsible for giving proper steering and engine orders for the safe navigation of a ship. This responsibility is usually exercised by the OOD
CPO	chief petty officer (a senior enlisted person)
CTF	Commander, task force ___
CV	aircraft carrier (ship type)
CVA	attack aircraft carrier (ship type)
CVAN	nuclear-powered attack aircraft carrier (ship type)
CVN	nuclear-powered aircraft carrier (ship type)
DCA	Defense Communications Agency or damage control assistant
DD	destroyer (ship type)
DDE	escort destroyer (ship type)
DDG	guided-missile destroyer (ship type)
DESRON	destroyer squadron
DLA	Defense Logistics Agency
DoD	Department of Defense
FF	frigate (ship type)
FFG	guided-missile frigate (ship type)
FY	fiscal year
GED	general equivalency degree (high-school level)
GWOT	global war on terrorism
HADR	humanitarian assistance and disaster relief
HBCU	historically black colleges and universities
IT	information technology
JAG Corps	Judge Advocate General's Corps
JCS	Joint Chiefs of Staff (made up of the top uniformed officers of each of the armed services)
JROTC	Junior Reserve Officer Training Corps
LHA	landing helicopter, assault (ship type)
LHD	landing helicopter dock (ship type)
LPD	amphibious transport dock (ship type)
LPH	landing platform, helicopter (ship type)
LSD	landing ship, dock (ship type)
LST	landing ship, tank (ship type)
MAA	master-at-arms
MOOTW	military operations other than war
MORE	Minority Officer Recruiting Effort
MSC	Military Sealift Command
NAACP	National Association for the Advancement of Colored People
NAE	Naval Aviation Enterprise
NAPS	Naval Academy Preparatory School
NATO	North Atlantic Treaty Organization
NAVEDTRACOM	Naval Education and Training Command
NDW	Naval District Washington

NFOC	Naval Flight Officer Candidate
NNOA	National Naval Officers Association
NROTC	Naval Reserve Officer Training Corps
NSA	National Security Agency
NTC	Naval Training Center
OASD	Office of the Assistant Secretary of Defense
OCS	Officer Candidate School
ONI	Office of Naval Intelligence
OOD	officer of the deck
PACEX	Pacific exercise
REDCOM	Readiness Command
RIMPAC	Rim of the Pacific (exercise)
RLSO	Region Legal Service Office
ROTC	Reserve Officer Training Corps
SEAL	sea, air, land (Navy special forces)
SLBM	submarine-launched ballistic missile
SPAWAR	Space and Naval Warfare Systems Command
SSBN	nuclear-powered ballistic-missile submarine (ship type)
SSGN	nuclear-powered guided-missile submarine (ship type)
SSN	nuclear attack submarine (ship type)
T-AH	hospital ship (ship type)
TF	task force ___
TRICARE	the military healthcare program
UN	United Nations
USACOM	U.S. Atlantic Command
USCENTCOM	U.S. Central Command
USMC	U.S. Marine Corps
USNA	U.S. Naval Academy ("Annapolis")
USNAVSO	U.S. Naval Forces, Southern Command
USPACOM	U.S. Pacific Command
USS	United States ship (designation for U.S. Navy vessels)
USSOUTHCOM	U.S. Southern Command
USSTRATCOM	U.S. Strategic Command
XO	executive officer (second in command)

Name	Date of Commission	Commissioning Source	Date of Flag Rank	Terminal Rank	Noteworthy Achievements as African Americans
Gravely, Samuel L. Jr.	1944	V-12 NROTC Program, UCLA	July 1, 1972	Vice admiral	First admiral
Thomas, Gerald E.	1951	NROTC	June 1, 1975	Rear admiral	Second admiral. Second NROTC admiral
Chambers, Lawrence C.	1952	USNA	August 1, 1977	Rear admiral	Second USNA graduate. First USNA graduate to achieve flag rank
Williams, Louis	1954	NROTC	July 1, 1979	Rear admiral	First flight instructor
Johnson, Wendell Norman	1957	OCS	January 1, 1985	Rear admiral	
Hacker, Benjamin T.	1958	OCS	March 1, 1981	Rear admiral	
Toney, Robert Lee	1958	OCS	September 1, 1985	Rear admiral	
Powell, William E. Jr.	1959	USNA	October 17, 1985	Rear admiral	First Supply Corps admiral
Davis, Walter	1959	NROTC, Ohio St. Univ.	December 1, 1988	Vice admiral	
Penn, B. J. "Buddie"	1961	AOCS	Retired August 1, 1982	Captain	First acting Secretary of the Navy
Fussell, Macea E.	1961	Ensign 1915 Prog.	November 1, 1992	Rear admiral	
Gaston, Mack C.	1964	OCS	1990	Rear admiral	
Reason, Joseph Paul	1965	USNA	October 1, 1987	Admiral	First 4-star admiral
Tzomes, C. A. 'Pete'	1966	USNA	Retired March 1, 1987	Captain	First submarine CO
Johnson, James A.	1966	Direct appointment (Ensign 1915 Program)	February 1, 2000	Rear admiral	First active-duty Medical Corps officer
Poe, Larry L.	1967	AOCS	March 1, 1996	Rear admiral	
Moore, Edward Jr.	1968	NROTC, Southern Illinois Univ., Carbondale	April 1, 1994	Vice admiral	First commander, surface forces, Pacific Fleet
Watson, Anthony	1970	USNA	October 1, 1994	Rear admiral	First submarine admiral
Brewer, David L. III	1970	NROTC, Prairie View A&M Univ., TX	October 1, 1995	Vice admiral	First amphibious group commander

(continued)

Name	Date of Commission	Commissioning Source	Date of Flag Rank	Terminal Rank	Noteworthy Achievements as African Americans
Combs, Osie V.	1971	NROTC, Prairie View A&M Univ., TX	September 1, 1996	Rear admiral	First engineering duty officer admiral
Kendall, Gene	1971	Nuclear Engineering Commissioning Prog., Univ. of Kansas	August 1, 1997	Rear admiral	
Robinson, Adam M. Jr.	1972	Armed Forces Health Professions Scholarship Prog., Southern Illinois Univ.	October 1, 2004	Vice admiral	First surgeon general of the armed forces
Fishburne, Lillian E.	1973	OCS	February 1, 1998	Rear admiral	First female flag officer
Marsh, Willie C.	1973	Army ROTC, Alabama A&M Univ.	September 1, 2000	Rear admiral	
Smith, Vinson E.	1974	NFOC Prog.	June 1, 2001	Rear admiral	
Bundy, William F.	1975	OCS	Retired September 1, 1994	Commander	First prior enlisted submarine commander
Bookert, Reubin B.	1975	OCS	October 1, 2002	Rear admiral	
Black, Barry C.	1976	Direct commission	February 1, 1998	Rear admiral	First chief of Navy chaplains
Curtis, Derwood	1976	USNA	September 1, 2003	Vice admiral	
Caesar, Julius S.	1977	USNA	October 1, 2008	Rear admiral	
Winns, Anthony L.	1978	USNA	March 1, 2002	Vice admiral	
Williams, Melvin G. Jr.	1978	USNA	October 1, 2003	Vice admiral	First SSBN CO. First submarine vice admiral. First fleet commander.
Haney, Cecil D.	1978	USNA	July 1, 2005	Admiral	Second four-star admiral
Guillory, Victor G.	1978	USNA	October 1, 2005	Rear admiral	
Johnson, Arthur J.	1979	USNA	October 1, 2004	Rear admiral	
Gay, Earl L.	1980	USNA	August 1, 2007	Rear admiral	
Grooms, Bruce E.	1980	USNA	June 1, 2007	Vice admiral	First USNA commandant of midshipmen

Name	Year	Commissioning Source	Date	Rank	Notes
Peterson, Joseph P.	1980	OCS	Retired July 31, 2013	Captain	
Dixon, Kelvin N.	1981	NROTC, Prairie View A&M Univ, TX	August 1, 2010	Rear admiral	
Harris, Sinclair	1981	OCS	July 30, 2009	Rear admiral	
Hayes, Norman R.	1982	OCS	July 1, 2008	Rear admiral	
Griffith, Vincent L.	1982	OCS	June 1, 2009	Rear admiral	
Howard, Michelle	1982	USNA	August 1, 2009	Admiral	First woman to command a warship. First Vice CNO
Carodine, Charles K.	1982	USNA	February 2, 2010	Rear admiral	
Scott, Kevin D.	1982	AOCS	June 1, 2010	Rear admiral	
Smith, John W.	1982	AOCS	September 1, 2011	Rear admiral	
Wilson, Jesse A. Jr.	1982	USNA	August 1, 2015	Rear admiral	
Crawford, James W. III	1983	Direct appointment	December 22, 2010	Rear admiral	
Andrews, Annie B.	1983	NROTC, Savannah St. Coll., GA	March 1, 2012	Rear admiral	
Ponds, Fernandez	1983	OCS	February 1, 2013	Rear admiral	
Shepherd, Dwight D.	1984	NFOC Prog.	April 1, 2013	Rear admiral	
Metts, Willie L.	1985	NROTC, Savannah St. Coll., GA	July 1, 2011	Rear admiral	
Young, Eric C.	1985	OCS	August 1, 2012	Rear admiral	
Evans, Stephen C.	1986	NROTC, The Citadel, SC	July 1, 2015	Rear admiral	
Holsey, Alvin	1988	NROTC, Morehouse Coll., GA	May 1, 2017	Rear admiral	

Primary source: David Lanham, Branch Head, Career Progression Eligibility Branch, PERS-802

ABOUT THE AUTHOR

Lieutenant Commander Robert Crosby is a graduate of the U.S. Naval War College, where he earned a Master of Arts degree in national security and strategic studies. He is a nuclear submarine officer.

Lieutenant Commander Crosby was reared in Hot Coffee, Mississippi, in the Mississippi Delta, the poorest region of the poorest state in America. As a youth, no one in his inner circle possessed a high school diploma, and his greatest mentor during this time possessed a fourth-grade education. Enlisting in the Navy as a cook afforded him the opportunity to receive a college education, two master's degrees, and a Capitol Hill assignment, while pursuing a career as a nuclear submarine officer. He completed sea tours in USS *Hampton* (SSN 767) and USS *Rhode Island* (SSBN 740).

Lieutenant Commander Crosby's inspirational story has been shared across the nation by the Navy, including in local newspapers and the Navy's *All Hands* magazine. Crosby wrote *My Journey from Hot Coffee to Scrambled Eggs to Nuclear Submarines,* as well as this paper, to inspire underserved youth. He is the founder of a nonprofit organization called BOOST—Broadened Opportunity for Outstanding Student Selection and Tracking. This program selects, tracks, and mentors high-performing students in underserved communities and "boosts" them beyond their environments to achieve their maximum potential. Crosby hopes to demonstrate that the Navy can not only fight and win wars but also can change lives.

Crosby became interested in the stories of Vice Admiral Samuel L. Gravely Jr. and his successors because of shared themes that revolve around beginning in meager circumstances, overcoming obstacles, and advancing in the Navy with the assistance of others. Crosby's story mimics the themes of the struggles of Gravely and his successors to overcome racism and social, economic, and workplace exclusion to make positive contributions to national defense. The author's message of using "A&W"—attitude and work ethic—to advance in careers that require specialized training and credentialing is enduring and is relevant now and will continue its relevance into the twenty-first century and beyond.

NOTES

1. www.history.navy.mil/. Incidentally, I later would have direct contact with then-Senator John Chafee when I was director of the Rhode Island Department of Transportation. Senator Chafee was as adamant about addressing discrimination then as he had been while serving as secretary.
2. www.history.navy.mil/.
3. Vice Adm. Samuel Gravely Jr., with Paul Stillwell, *Trailblazer: The U.S. Navy's First Black Admiral* (Annapolis, MD: Naval Institute Press, 2010).
4. "Samuel L. Gravely Jr.," *National Visionary Leadership Project—Visionary Videos,* www.visionary project.org/.
5. Ibid.
6. Gail Lumet Buckley, *American Patriots: The Story of Blacks in the Military from the Revolution to Desert Storm* (New York: Random House, 2002), p. xvii.
7. Alma Gravely, interview by author, February 1, 2014.
8. Gravely with Stillwell, *Trailblazer,* p. 6.
9. Quoted in Akers, "Vice Adm. Samuel L. Gravely, Jr."
10. "The Value of Mentoring," *MENTOR: The National Mentoring Partnership,* www.mentoring.org/.
11. Public/private ventures study of big brothers big sisters, *MENTOR: The National Mentoring Partnership,* www.mentoring.org/.
12. Ibid.
13. Ibid.
14. Pamela Barnett, "Navy Rear Admiral," *about careers,* usmilitary.about.com/.
15. Cdr. Jim Jackson, USN (Ret.), "The Navy's Black Admirals," *Black Bars to Gold Stripes,* www.black navyadmirals.com/.
16. Desiree D. Linson, *Vice Admiral Samuel Gravely: Leadership by Example* (graduate thesis, Air Command and Staff College, 1998), p. iv, available at mafb-primo.hosted.exlibrisgroup.com/.
17. Gravely interview.
18. Gravely with Stillwell, *Trailblazer,* pp. 2–3.
19. Linson, *Vice Admiral Samuel Gravely,* p. 5.
20. Ibid.
21. Ibid., p. 6.
22. Lt. Dennis D. Nelson, *The Integration of the Negro into the U.S. Navy* (New York: Farrar, Straus, and Young, 1951), p. 9.
23. Gravely with Stillwell, *Trailblazer,* pp. 7–8, 12.
24. Gravely interview.
25. Linson, *Vice Admiral Samuel Gravely,* p. 10.
26. Navy Commendation Medal covering the period March–April 1968.
27. Meritorious Service Medal covering the period September 1968–April 1970.
28. Legion of Merit covering the period July 1971–June 1973.
29. Legion of Merit covering the period September 1976–September 1978.

30. "About—Our History: The 1980s," *DISA: Defense Information Systems Agency, the IT Combat Support Agency,* www.disa.mil/.

31. David A. Fritz et al., "Military Satellite Communications: Space-Based Communication for the Global Information Grid," *Johns Hopkins APL Technical Digest* 27, no. 1 (2006), available at techdigest.jhuapl.edu/.

32. Defense Distinguished Service Medal covering the period September 1978–July 1980.

33. Matthew G. Washington, "Thomas, Gerald E.," *BlackPast.org.*

34. Navy Commendation Medal covering the period May–October 1967.

35. Meritorious Service Medal covering the period July 1969–July 1970.

36. Legion of Merit covering the period December 1978–July 1981.

37. Rick Rogers, "Louis Williams," *San Diego Union-Tribune,* May 26, 2008, available at www.sandiego uniontribune.com/.

38. Letter of Commendation covering the period February–May 1965.

39. Joint Service Commendation Medal covering the period April–September 1975.

40. Tom Long, "Wendell Norman Johnson, BU Dean, Rear Admiral; 72," *Boston Globe,* May 7, 2007, available at www.boston.com/.

41. Navy Commendation Medal covering the period November 1965–February 1966.

42. Letter of Commendation covering the period July 1968–December 1969.

43. Meritorious Service medal covering the period July 1971–July 1974.

44. Meritorious Service Medal covering the period April 1979–October 1981. (Note: the citation for this award reads "William Norman Johnson.")

45. Legion of Merit covering the period October 1983–December 1986.

46. "Center Commanders: Rear Adm. Benjamin T. Hacker," www.quarterdeck.org/.

47. Letter of Commendation covering the period October–December 1962.

48. Legion of Merit covering the period August 1978–August 1980.

49. Legion of Merit covering the period July 1982–August 1984.

50. Legion of Merit covering the period August 1986–May 1988.

51. Rear Adm. Toney, oral history by author, September 25, 2014.

52. Meritorious Service Medal covering the period December 1969–August 1972.

53. Legion of Merit covering the period January 1986–November 1988.

54. Defense Distinguished Service Medal covering the period February 1989–January 1991.

55. Rear Adm. Frank J. Allston, USNR (Ret.), *Ready for Sea: The Bicentennial History of the U.S. Navy Supply Corps* (Annapolis, MD: Naval Institute Press, 1995), excerpted in "Lore of the Corps," *The Free Library,* available at www.thefreelibrary.com/.

56. Ibid.

57. Simeon Booker, "Ticker Tape U.S.A.," JET, July 28, 1986, p. 10, available at books.google.com/.

58. Lt. Reid Morrow, SC, USN, "Supply Corps Names Library after Retired Rear Admiral Powell Jr.," *The Oakleaf* (June 2013), p. 11, available at www.usnscf.com/.

59. Meritorious Service Medal covering the period June 1980–May 1982.

60. Legion of Merit covering the period June 1982–June 1984.

61. Legion of Merit covering the period May 1985–October 1988.

62. Vice Adm. Walter Davis, interview by author, October 18, 2014.

63. Vice Adm. Walter Davis, interview by author, October 17, 2014.

64. Ibid.

65. Ibid.

66. Ibid.

67. Ibid.

68. Ibid.

69. Rear Adm. Macea Fussell, interview by author, September 20, 2014.

70. Meritorious Service Medal covering the period October 1987–September 1990.

71. Meritorious Service Medal covering the period October 1991–September 1993.

72. Legion of Merit covering the period July 1993–August 1995.

73. Rear Adm. Mack Gaston, interview by author, May 14, 2015.

74. Meritorious Service Medal covering the period September 1984–August 1985.

75. Defense Superior Service Medal covering the period June 1990–July 1992.
76. Defense Distinguished Service Medal covering the period August 1992–May 1995.
77. Wikipedia, s.v. "J. Paul Reason," en.wikipedia.org/.
78. Michael Watkins, "Reason, J. Paul 1943," *Contemporary Black Biography* (Farmington Hills, MI: Thomson Gale, 1999), excerpted in Encyclopedia.com.
79. Navy Commendation Medal covering the period September–December 1972.
80. Legion of Merit covering the period January 1977–June 1979.
81. Legion of Merit covering the period July 1986–September 1988.
82. Distinguished Service Medal covering the period January 1991–May 1994.
83. Distinguished Service Medal covering the period December 1996–September 1999.
84. Rear Adm. James Johnson, interview by author, December 15, 2015.
85. Navy Commendation Medal covering the period March 1983–October 1989.
86. Meritorious Service Medal covering the period October 1989–June 1991.
87. Meritorious Service Medal covering the period July 1991–March 1994.
88. Legion of Merit covering the period October 1994–August 1997.
89. Rear Adm. Larry Poe, interview by author, September 22, 2014.
90. Defense Superior Service Medal covering the period February 1996–July 1999.
91. Legion of Merit covering the period May–November 1997.
92. Poe interview.
93. Ibid.
94. Ibid.
95. Vice Adm. Edward Moore, interview by author, July 14, 2014.
96. Meritorious Service Medal covering the period August 1984–October 1986.
97. Legion of Merit covering the period November 1986–June 1989.
98. Legion of Merit covering the period June 1989–February 1993.
99. Legion of Merit covering the period July 1995–December 1996.
100. Legion of Merit covering the period January 1997–July 1998.
101. Distinguished Service Medal covering the period August 1998–May 2001.
102. Vice Adm. David Brewer, interview by author, August 20, 2014.
103. Navy Achievement Medal covering the period February–May 1977.
104. Meritorious Service Medal covering the period June 1986–September 1988.
105. Meritorious Service Medal covering the period September 1988–January 1991.
106. Defense Superior Service Medal covering the period August 1994–December 1996.
107. Legion of Merit covering the period January 1997–January 1999.
108. Legion of Merit covering the period March 1999–August 2001.
109. Distinguished Service Medal covering the period August 2001–March 2006.
110. Rear Adm. Osie Combs, interview by author, March 14, 2014.
111. Meritorious Service Medal covering the period April 1985–March 1988.
112. Meritorious Service Medal covering the period April 1988–July 1990.
113. Legion of Merit covering the period March 1995–June 1998.
114. Rear Adm. Gene Kendall, interview by author, June 1, 2014.
115. Meritorious Service Medal covering the period November 1988–December 1990.
116. Defense Superior Service Medal covering the period August 1996–December 1997.
117. Legion of Merit covering the period April 1998–July 2000.
118. Vice Adm. Adam Robinson, interview by author, May 7, 2014.
119. Navy Achievement Medal covering the period March 1983–May 1984.
120. Navy Commendation Medal covering the period October 1985–August 1990.
121. Legion of Merit covering the period August 2001–January 2004.
122. Defense Meritorious Service Medal covering the period January–July 1999.
123. Meritorious Service Medal covering the period August 1999–August 2000.
124. Distinguished Service Medal covering the period February 2009–November 2011.
125. Rear Adm. Lillian Fishburne, interview by author, September 10, 2014.
126. Gold Wreath Award covering the period January–March 1977.
127. Meritorious Service Medal covering the period March 1987–June 1990.

128. Legion of Merit covering the period August 1995–October 1997.
129. Legion of Merit covering the period May 1998–October 2000.
130. Rear Adm. Willie Marsh, interview by author, November 10, 2014.
131. Meritorious Service Medal covering the period April 1987–July 1989.
132. Legion of Merit covering the period November 1996–August 1998.
133. Bronze Star covering the period January–May 2003.
134. "Rear Admiral Vinson E. Smith Retired," *America's Navy: United States Navy Biography*, www.navy.mil/.
135. Meritorious Service Medal covering the period September 1994–September 1995.
136. Legion of Merit covering the period February 1996–May 1999.
137. Legion of Merit covering the period August 2000–August 2002.
138. Rear Adm. Reubin Bookert, interview by author, October 10, 2014.
139. Meritorious Service Medal for the period covering July 1994.
140. Legion of Merit for the period covering July 1995–July 1996.
141. Legion of Merit for the period covering February 2001–July 2003.
142. Rear Adm. Barry Black, interview by author, October 5, 2014.
143. Legion of Merit covering the period July 1994–August 1997.
144. Defense Meritorious Service Medal covering the period August 2000–June 2001.
145. Distinguished Service Medal covering the period August 2000–August 2003.
146. Vice Adm. Derwood Curtis, interview by author, September 9, 2014.
147. Meritorious Service Medal covering the period December 1993–May 1994.
148. Vice Adm. Derwood Curtis, interview by author, May 25, 2014.
149. Defense Meritorious Service Medal covering the period August 1996–June 1998.
150. Legion of Merit covering the period October 1998–April 2000.
151. Legion of Merit covering the period January 2001–August 2002.
152. Legion of Merit covering the period September 2002–February 2004.
153. Legion of Merit covering the period February 2004–February 2005.
154. Legion of Merit covering the period June 2005–June 2006.
155. Distinguished Service Medal covering the period March 2008–June 2011.
156. Rear Adm. Julius Caesar, interview by author, August 13, 2014.
157. Meritorious Service Medal covering the period October 2000–September 2002.
158. Meritorious Service Medal covering the period October 1998–September 2000.
159. Legion of Merit covering the period October 2004–September 2005.
160. Defense Superior Service Medal covering the period December 2010–September 2011.
161. Vice Adm. Anthony Winns, interview by author, July 30, 2014.
162. Navy Commendation Medal covering the period January 1984–December 1985.
163. Navy Commendation Medal covering the period February 1991–March 1992.
164. Meritorious Service Medal covering the period August 1994–March 1995.
165. Legion of Merit covering the period December 1996–November 1998.
166. Legion of Merit covering the period June 2001–September 2003.
167. Legion of Merit covering the period September 2003–August 2005.
168. Defense Superior Service Medal covering the period August 2005–August 2007.
169. Distinguished Service Medal covering the period February 2009–April 2011.
170. Rear Adm. Victor Guillory, interview by author, June 23, 2014.
171. Navy Commendation Medal covering the period July 3, 1988.
172. Legion of Merit covering the period February 2000–October 2001.
173. Legion of Merit covering the period October 2007–June 2009.
174. Distinguished Service Medal covering the period June 2009–August 2011.
175. Rear Adm. Arthur Johnson, interview by author, December 15, 2015.
176. Navy Commendation Medal covering the period July 1994–May 1995.
177. Meritorious Service Medal covering the period September 1997–June 1999.
178. Legion of Merit covering the period October 2000–April 2002.
179. Rear Adm. Earl Gay, interview by author, November 1, 2014.
180. Meritorious Service Medal covering the period October 1996–February 1998.

181. Legion of Merit covering the period August 2007–July 2008.
182. Legion of Merit covering the period July 2009–July 2011.
183. Rear Adm. Kelvin Dixon, interview by author, October 9, 2014.
184. Meritorious Service Medal covering the period October 1998–September 2000.
185. Meritorious Service Medal covering the period October 2002–September 2004.
186. Meritorious Service Medal covering the period October 2004–September 2006.
187. Defense Superior Service Medal covering the period August 2010–December 2011.
188. Rear Adm. Sinclair Harris, interview by author, July 24, 2014.
189. Ibid.
190. Legion of Merit covering the period February 2002–September 2004.
191. Defense Meritorious Service Medal covering the period July 2007–June 2008.
192. Legion of Merit covering the period May 2008–September 2009.
193. Legion of Merit covering the period November 2009–November 2010.
194. Legion of Merit covering the period December 2010–May 2012.
195. Rear Adm. Norman Hayes, interview by author, March 12, 2014.
196. Defense Meritorious Service Medal covering the period September 1996–September 1999.
197. Meritorious Service Medal covering the period July 2000–June 2002.
198. Legion of Merit covering the period June 2007–September 2008.
199. Rear Adm. Vincent Griffith, interview by author, June 24, 2014.
200. Meritorious Service Medal covering the period October 2000–April 2002.
201. Legion of Merit covering the period August 2006–June 2009.
202. Defense Superior Service Medal covering the period June 2009–June 2011.
203. Legion of Merit covering the period September 2011–July 2013.
204. Adm. Michelle Howard, interview by author, August 20, 2014.
205. Bradley Olson, "Rear Admiral-to-be Always a Trailblazer," *Baltimore Sun*, August 22, 2006, available at articles.baltimoresun.com/.
206. Navy Commendation Medal covering the period December 1993–August 1995.
207. Navy Commendation Medal covering the period March 1986–May 1987.
208. Navy Commendation Medal covering the period November 1990–May 1992.
209. Meritorious Service Medal covering the period March 1999–November 2000.
210. Legion of Merit covering the period May 2004–September 2005.
211. Legion of Merit covering the period April 2009–July 2010.
212. Rear Adm. Charles Carodine, interview by author, August 23, 2014.
213. Meritorious Service Medal covering the period October 2000–September 2002.
214. Meritorious Service Medal covering the period October 2005–December 2006.
215. Legion of Merit covering the period February 2010–June 2012.
216. Legion of Merit covering the period June 2012–March 2013.
217. Rear Adm. Kevin Scott, interview by author, August 24, 2014.
218. Legion of Merit covering the period July 2005–August 2007.
219. Legion of Merit covering the period August 2007–August 2009.
220. Legion of Merit covering the period September 2009–July 2010.
221. Legion of Merit covering the period July 2010–March 2012.
222. Rear Adm. John Smith, interview by author, April 20, 2014.
223. Meritorious Service Medal covering the period July 2001–November 2002.
224. Legion of Merit covering the period November 2005–June 2007.
225. Meritorious Service Medal covering the period January 2003–December 2004.
226. Meritorious Service Medal covering the period November 2009–July 2010.
227. Joint Service Achievement Medal covering the period September 2001–October 2001.
228. Meritorious Service Medal covering the period November 2004–November 2006.
229. Legion of Merit covering the period August 2007–December 2008.
230. Legion of Merit covering the period December 2010–May 2012.
231. Defense Superior Service Medal covering the period July 2014–November 2015.
232. Legion of Merit covering the period November 2015–September 2016.
233. Legion of Merit covering the period September 2016–July 2017.

234. Rear Adm. James Crawford, interview by author, April 19, 2016.

235. Meritorious Service Medal covering the period June 1997–June 1999.

236. Legion of Merit covering the period August 2005–March 2007.

237. Defense Superior Service Medal covering the period October 2007–September 2011.

238. Defense Superior Service Medal covering the period September 2011–September 2012.

239. Rear Adm. Annie Andrews, interview by author, February 15, 2014.

240. Defense Meritorious Service Medal covering the period June 1995–July 1998.

241. Navy Commendation Medal covering the period December 1992–May 1995.

242. Defense Meritorious Service Medal covering the period September 1999–September 2001.

243. Meritorious Service Medal covering the period June 2002–April 2005.

244. Rear Adm. Fernandez Ponds, interview by author, November 3, 2015.

245. Meritorious Service Medal covering the period September 1998–April 2000.

246. Meritorious Service Medal covering the period August–November 2008.

247. Legion of Merit covering the period September 2010–October 2011.

248. Rear Adm. Dwight Shepherd, interview by author, August 19, 2014.

249. Meritorious Service Medal covering the period July 2002–July 2003.

250. Meritorious Service Medal covering the period September 2003–March 2005.

251. Legion of Merit covering the period June 2007–August 2010.

252. Rear Adm. Willie Metts, interview by author, July 24, 2014.

253. Legion of Merit covering the period July 2005–June 2006.

254. Legion of Merit covering the period July 2006–July 2008.

255. Defense Superior Service Medal covering the period August 2011–June 2013.

256. Rear Adm. Eric Young, interview by author, July 23, 2014.

257. Navy Achievement Medal covering the period April–June 1987.

258. Meritorious Service Medal covering the period November 1999 to July 2001.

259. Meritorious Service Medal covering the period August 2005–November 2007.

260. Legion of Merit covering the period June 2009–November 2010.

261. Defense Superior Service Medal covering the period April 2011–July 2012.

262. Admiral Holsey to author, May 19, 2017.

263. Legion of Merit covering the period February 2012–December 2014.

264. Admiral Holsey to author, May 19, 2017.

265. "How Did Capt. Pete Tzomes Make History in the Submarine Community?" *All Hands Online,* February 26, 2013, newsmilitary.com/.

266. Patrick House, "Breaking the Barrier: The Story of the Navy's First African American Submarine Commanding Officer," All Hands, 8 March 8, 2013, www.navy.mil/.

267. Tzomes, nomination package for Black Engineer of the Year Award (in award citation packet).

268. Capt. C. A. Tzomes, interview by author, June 6, 2014.

269. Meritorious Service Medal covering the period December 1987–November 1989.

270. Legion of Merit covering the period June 1992–July 1993.

271. Defense Superior Service Medal covering the period August 1993–June 1995.

272. William Bundy, oral history, *The HistoryMakers: The Nation's Largest African American Video Oral History Collection,* April 27, 2013, www.thehistorymakers.com/.

273. Defense Meritorious Service Medal covering the period March 1981–March 1984.

274. Dr. William Bundy, interview by author, May 1, 2014.

275. Ibid.

276. Ibid.

277. Melvin G. Williams and Melvin G. Williams Jr., *Navigating the Seven Seas: Leadership Lessons of the First African American Father and Son to Serve at the Top in the U.S. Navy* (Annapolis, MD: Naval Institute Press, 2011).

278. "Vice Admiral Melvin G. 'Mel' Williams, Jr. Commander, U.S. Second Fleet," *America's Navy: United States Navy Biography,* www.navy.mil/.

279. Defense Meritorious Service Medal covering the period December 1982–June 1984.

280. Navy Commendation Medal covering the period November 1984–February 1987.

281. Navy Commendation Medal covering the period October 1989–December 1991.

282. Legion of Merit covering the period August 1994–June 1997.
283. Legion of Merit covering the period July 1997–January 1999.
284. Legion of Merit covering the period April 1999–September 2000.
285. Capt. Melvin Williams Jr., interview by author, August 22, 2014.
286. Legion of Merit covering the period October 2000–July 2002.
287. Legion of Merit covering the period February 2003–June 2005.
288. Distinguished Service Medal covering the period August 2008–August 2010.
289. Capt. Cecil D. Haney, interview by author, March 2, 2014.
290. Navy Commendation Medal covering the period August 1983–July 1985.
291. Navy Achievement Medal covering the period September 1989–January 1990.
292. Legion of Merit covering the period June 1996–May 1999.
293. Defense Superior Service Medal covering the period June 2000–May 2002.
294. Legion of Merit covering the period July 2002–July 2004.
295. Distinguished Service Medal covering the period March 2008–October 2010.
296. Legion of Merit covering the period July 2004–August 2006.
297. Adm. Cecil D. Haney, interview by author, May 14, 2014.
298. Defense Superior Service Medal covering the period October 2010–December 2011.
299. Vice Adm. Bruce Grooms, interview by author, March 2, 2014.
300. Navy Achievement Medal covering the period February 1986–July 1988.
301. Bradley Olson, "Commandant's Leadership Could Take Him to the Top," *Baltimore Sun,* December 10, 2005, available at articles.baltimoresun.com/.
302. Navy Commendation Medal covering the period May–August 1995.
303. Legion of Merit covering the period August 1997–October 1999.
304. Olson, "Commandant's Leadership Could Take Him to the Top."
305. Meritorious Service Medal covering the period November 1999–July 2001.
306. Adm. Bruce Grooms, interview by author, May 1, 2014.
307. Legion of Merit covering the period July 2003–May 2005.
308. Legion of Merit covering the period February 2007–March 2008.
309. Interview with Grooms, March 2, 2014.
310. Legion of Merit covering the period March 2008–May 2009.
311. Defense Superior Service Medal covering the period June 2009–November 2010.
312. Legion of Merit covering the period November 2010–March 2013.
313. Capt. Joseph Peterson, interview by author, March 3, 2014.
314. "USS Dolphin (AGSS 555)," globalsecurity.org.
315. Peterson interview.
316. Navy Commendation Medal covering the period June 1988–July 1990.
317. Legion of Merit covering the period October 2001–August 2004.
318. Rear Adm. Lawrence C. Chambers, interview by author, September 1, 2014.
319. Bronze Star Medal covering the period July–December 1970.
320. Meritorious Service Medal covering the period April–May 1975.
321. Legion of Merit covering the period November 1979–April 1981.
322. The Honorable Buddy Penn, interview by author, October 1, 2014.
323. Air Medal covering the period July 1972–January 1973.
324. Meritorious Service medal covering the period June 1985–June 1987.
325. Legion of Merit covering the period January 1982–June 1985.
326. Legion of Merit covering the period July 1987–June 1991.
327. Michael Hyatt, "Four Characteristics of Inspirational Leaders," *Michael Hyatt,* michaelhyatt.com/.